CRICKET AND EMPIRE

RIC SISSONS AND BRIAN STODDART

Cricket and Empire

The 1932-33 Bodyline tour of Australia

London
GEORGE ALLEN & UNWIN
Boston Sydney

This edition first published in Great Britain by
George Allen & Unwin (Publishers) Ltd 1984.

George Allen & Unwin (Publishers) Ltd
40 Museum Street, London WC1A 1LU, UK

George Allen & Unwin (Publishers) Ltd
Park Lane, Hemel Hempstead, Herts HP2 4TE UK

George Allen & Unwin Australia Pty Ltd
8 Napier Street, North Sydney NSW 2060 Australia

© Ric Sissons & Brian Stoddart 1984

ISBN 0 04 796090 6

Set in 10/12pt Plantin by Setrite Typesetters Ltd, Hong Kong
Printed in Great Britain by
Billing and Sons Ltd., London and Worcester

Contents

Illustrations

Acknowledgements

We would like to thank the following for making their time and information available to us and for the encouragement to continue: Gubby Allen, Bill Bowes, Freddy Brown, Richard Cashman, Brooke Crutchley, the families of H.W. Hodgetts and S.H.D. Rowe, Stephen Green, Gerald Howat, Robin Jeffrey, Fiannach Lawry, Dame Enid Lyons, Bill Mandle, Gilbert Mant, Herbert Mishael, Pat Mullins, Nip Pellew, David Puttnam, Peter Reeves, Tim Wall and Cliff Winning.

The book could not have been written without the resources, and the tireless assistance of the staff, of the Australian Archives, the Australian Cricket Board, the Australian National Library, the British Library, the British Museum Newspaper Library, the Marylebone Cricket Club Library, the New South Wales Cricket Association Library, the Public Records Office in London and the State Archives of South Australia. Brian Stoddart also acknowledges the financial support given him by the Australian Research Grants Committee from 1978 to 1980.

Obviously, none of the above are responsible for our conclusions. We can only hope that when they read the book they feel their time in talking to one or other of us was well spent.

For Sandi and Stephanie

Introduction

During the 1982–83 Australian summer, and cricket season, an old controversy was revived. In Australia and England, a renewed search began for the true character of a test cricket series played half a century earlier. The anniversary was partly the reason for the renewed interest; fiftieth anniversaries frequently are. In the case of the 1932–33 Marylebone Cricket Club (MCC) tour of Australia, however, there was more to it than a simple number of years past. Though the facts of that cricket visit have never been at issue, what has never been successfully resolved is its real meaning: how its events went far beyond the cricket ground fences and into the collective memory of an Anglo-Australian generation for whom cricket was a major cultural bond.

Fifty years on, then, the memories of old players were probed anew; old tour books were dusted off and some republished; old photographs were rediscovered; new books appeared; newspaper and newsreel archives endured numerous cricket researchers; radio and television documentaries were put in train, as were television and film projects of more elaborate scope; while English and Australian newspapers became crammed with stories about *the* tour.

This activity in itself testified to the significance of the 1932–33 series. Cricket has a long history and a large, devoted band of historians but, even so, most of its jubilees and centenaries pass unnoticed by the outside world. This is the case even in the all-important history of England versus Australia test matches. While the cricket world was enthralled by the one-hundredth anniversary tests played in both Australia and England during 1977–78, they occasioned only passing interest to an outside world in the midst of political crises, international conflict and economic gloom. Not so in 1982–83 when cricket history for a while ranked alongside more pressing preoccupations.

1

One case in point concerned a cricket incident in the schooldays of the man who went on to captain England in the 1932–33 series, D.R. Jardine. An article in the English *Observer* highlighted a story told about Jardine in a cricketing dictionary of biography written by a British MP, Ian Sproat. While at Winchester just after the First World War, the future England captain was said to have won an intra-school match by insisting on a recount of the scores, thereby displaying an unwarranted will to win. Moreover, this imperious attitude was said to have carried over into the boy's relationship with his teammates. In posting results of a match, he was said to have named only himself and another player, consigning the rest to oblivion on the grounds that they contributed nothing to the game. After this report, the *Observer* received numerous letters from Old Wykehamists (ex-Winchester men) denying, confirming or modifying the story.

Two important points arise from this spirited discussion. The incident itself was thought symbolically important in that it might shed further light on Jardine's personality, widely believed to be a major cause of the 1932–33 events in Australia. Indeed, it was not so much the accuracy of the story which was at stake as the character of an Old Wykehamist. This was uncannily close to the debates about character, behaviour and cricket which had occurred in England 50 years earlier. Secondly, the search for 'truth' in the Winchester affair revealed the extent of minute detail which investigators were prepared to pursue in order that they might uncover the 'real' bodyline story.

Yet despite all this reinvestigation, the true nature of the 1932–33 tour remains elusive. The major reason is that the emphasis has been largely upon the purely cricketing events which, while important, cannot explain the full range of emotions displayed at the time. Though some new material has been uncovered, by and large it has been placed in old frameworks so that the interpretations remain substantially as before. Other sources remain closed.

In this book the emphasis is rather upon the social and political context of the 1932–33 tour. In such a context, the cricket tour is shown to have played a major part in the working out of political and social relations between England and Australia in the later stages of the British Empire. Much of the ferocity raised by the tour has its explanation in the symbolic importance of cricket within the Empire, and much of its subsequent interest relates to the role of sport in modern society, especially the delicate matter of sport and politics. This approach has only just received wide acceptance. In 1977 one of the present authors, a professional historian, was awarded a small grant to begin ouch an interpretation and probe the evidence in an attempt to clarify some of the remaining mysteries. Immediate reactions to the announcement of the grant indicated a general desire to leave the bodyline controversy at rest. It had once threatened the Anglo-Australian connection, but all was now forgotten and should remain that way. The project was dismissed by letter-writers, radio contributors, columnists and journalists as, among other things, an addle-brained academic plot to waste public funds. A question about the financing of the project was even asked in the Australian Senate. One well-known Perth columnist, the late Kirwin Ward, summed it all up: 'Lord only knows what's left to research about bodyline. No controversy in sporting history has ever been so exhaustively covered, so remorselessley analysed, so boringly discussed, and endlessly written about.'

Six years later, Ward would have been dismayed and puzzled by the earnestness attached to the investigation of bodyline. As a fair-minded commentator and cricket enthusiast, though, he would have delighted in the revelations so produced. He would also have appreciated the need for access to as yet unavailable vital evidence in order to complete the story. This book cannot be definitive in the absence of that material—but it *is* the most complete analysis yet, and unique in its placing of bodyline in a social and political context. In that, it goes further than any other available work towards explaining both the passions aroused by bodyline in its own time, and its political lessons for ours.

1
The bodyline story

Superficially, the 1932–33 tour story is quite simple. In an itinerary of 22 official matches the MCC won ten, drew ten, tied one and lost one—an excellent record by an standards. More to the point, the MCC won the all-important test series four to one and so regained the 'Ashes', that symbol of power contested between what were then cricket's two most powerful nations. It was a heady result for English cricket, avenging the 1930 series loss and repeating the four-to-one victory for England in 1928–29. The 1932–33 test matches resulted for England thus: first test (Sydney) won by 10 wickets; second test (Melbourne) lost by 111 runs; third test (Adelaide) won by 338 runs; fourth test (Brisbane) won by 6 wickets; fifth test (Sydney) won by 8 wickets. However, it was the *means* by which those results were achieved, rather than the results themselves, which caused all the uproar.

England won by way of a major departure in fast bowling strategy. The English fast bowlers aimed on or outside the batsmen's leg stumps, and considerably short of a good length. That meant the deliveries came at the Australian batsmen fast, high and in line with their bodies. A 5½ ounce leather ball moving at approximately 90 miles (about 145 km) per hour would have been frightening enough under those circumstances, but the field placings which supported the English bowlers placed further restrictions upon the Australians. When this attack was used the batsmen had three options: to duck, thereby being unable to score runs; if unable to duck, to allow the ball to hit their bodies and so risk serious injury; or to play at the ball more in self-defence than attack. Field placings largely foreclosed the last option. The fielders were placed in clusters on the legside, mostly behind the batsmen, with inner and outer rings. If the batsman played a shot, he was invariably dismissed caught.

The bodyline story

The Australian players never devised a viable counter to the English onslaught, and many suffered fearful body blows trying to stand their ground without risking shots. Those injuries, and an apparent helplessness against the English methods, turned the Australian public against the visitors so that many ugly scenes of discontent, even hatred, eventuated.

Bowling to a leg side field was not new. Known as leg theory, its history dated from the later nineteenth century and had been employed by English bowlers such as Fred Root during periods when good pitches allowed batsmen to dominate bowlers. However, these earlier versions were used largely to restrict scoring rather than take wickets, and mainly by slow and medium pace bowlers who bowled on a length rather than short, so that batsmen were in little or no danger of being hit. The 1932–33 innovation was that fast bowlers adopted the method, and bowled very short in an attempt to dismiss rather than restrict batsmen. It was devastatingly successful so far as results were concerned.

A new word emerged to describe these tactics—bodyline. It originated as a telegraphic shorthand for 'line of the body', describing graphically the essential feature of the English bowling. Like the tactics themselves, the creator of the term is not known. Its most likely originator was Hugh Buggy. He was then with the Melbourne *Herald*, later spent many years as a 'crusading' journalist with publications like *Truth*, and had close contact with Melbourne's legendary sporting and underworld character, John Wren. Unfortunately, the few personal papers left by Buggy (now in the La Trobe Library, Melbourne) throw no light on the 1932–33 episode. Claude Corbett was another sportswriter often connected with 'bodyline'. Corbett was then with the Sydney *Sun*, but came from the redoubtable family most connected with the *Referee*, arguably Australia's best-ever sports paper. Jack Worrall, a famous old-time writer for the *Australasian*, is credited by the *Macquarie Dictionary* with having invented the word. However, Gilbert Mant (Reuter's correspondent on the tour) is of the opinion that Claude Corbett credited Hugh Buggy with the telegraphese.

Whatever its provenance, bodyline became one of the most emotive of English words. In its precise meaning of a bowling theory it gained official recognition in the *Concise Oxford Dictionary*, while in the colloquial it became synonomous with anything underhand. During the tour, it helped consign the British image in Australia to one of its lowest points ever. It became part of popular culture, where so many public attitudes find their most evocative expression. At the height of the controversy a verse was added to a music hall song, sympathising with the Australian plight:

> Now this new kind of cricket,
> Takes courage to stick it,
> There's bruises and fractures galore.
> After kissing their wives
> And insuring their lives
> Batsmen fearfully walk out to score.
> With a prayer and a curse
> They prepare for the hearse,
> Undertakers look on with broad grins.
> Oh, they'd be a lot calmer
> In Ned Kelly's armor,
> When Larwood, the wrecker, begins.

In such an atmosphere it was not surprising that Larwood (the English bowler mentioned above) should overhear a small child's remark: 'Why, Mummy, he doesn't *look* like a murderer!'; or that his railway carriage was invaded by irate Australians in a small Queensland town. These same high passions resulted in crowd demonstrations all over Australia and in all sections of the cricket grounds; they saw Australia's crowd tradition of 'barracking' reach new and abusive heights, and created fears for the safety of the imperial relationship among diplomats and politicians.

In the midst of all of this drama it was and remains easy to overlook that the tour, like any other, produced its heroes and villains and memorable moments. The cricket, and the drama, were dominated by three main players: Douglas Robert Jardine, the English captain; Harold Larwood, the principal English fast bowler; and Australia's Donald George Bradman, one of the world's best-ever batsmen.

Jardine marked a change in the conventions of English captaincy. Like all English captains until the early 1950s he was an amateur, a gentleman with sufficient means to allow him to play cricket for recreational rather than monetary purpose. In the 1930s this 'amateur

6

versus professional' strain in English cricket was still very strong—
'gentlemen' and 'players' still used separate dressing rooms and, on
some grounds, separate gates out to the playing field. But Jardine was
an amateur who played the game hard, almost like a professional whose
financial future depended upon success. As a tour leader he was a direct
contrast to most of his predecessors, such as A.E.R. Gilligan who led
the 1924–25 tour and A.P.F. Chapman that of 1928–29. Unlike them,
cricket for Jardine was the reason for the tour, with public relations and
diplomatic sociability ranking as a very distant second priority.

Sociability and personal charm were Gilligan's great attributes. To
fellow players he was always affable, to cricket lovers always
enthusiastic and interesting. Gilligan visited Australia many times subsequently as a commentator, and modern English writer John
Woodcock records that on one occasion a Sydney taxi driver, 'in a harsh
Australian accent', refused to charge the Englishman he had most
wanted to meet. Monty Noble, one of Australia's most famous players,
summed it up: in 'days of national unsettlement and disruptive
influences generally, Gilligan proved himself a splendid ambassador
for his country'. The importance placed upon sociability by English
authorities was noticeable in the circumstances of Gilligan's selection.
He was a leading fast bowler until he suffered a serious injury during
the 1924 English season. Though virtually a playing 'passenger', he
still led the side to Australia the following English winter. His modest
tactical and considerable social skills guaranteed him the trip.

Percy Chapman was, if anything, even more attractive, agreeable and
diplomatic. When he died in 1961, *The Times* obituary paid an
eloquent tribute:

> Some may cavil that he was a persuasive charmer rather than a
> stern disciplinarian, that his leadership owed more to the vivacity
> of his personality than to the subtle study of tactics—even that he
> was too lighthearted. But a generation that has seen too much
> unrelenting warfare on the first-class field will remember with
> relish the gaiety of his approach, the uninhibited vigour of his
> batting and the glamour of his fielding. There was sunlight in his
> cricket.

He was more fortunate than Gilligan in that the Australian line-up was
undergoing some changes while his own was at full strength—the result

of 1924–25 was reversed. Walter Hammond created a record for England which still stands—905 in the series with an average of 113.12. Chapman himself scored 50 in the first test but, like his predecessors, was not a great performer—he finished his test career of 36 innings with an average of 28.90, one century and five half-centuries. A brilliant fielder, he took 32 catches in his 26 matches; Hammond considered that Chapman's magnificent catch to dismiss Woodfull in the first test lifted the Englishmen for the whole series.

Chapman was an attacking player; he often 'appeared to sacrifice himself in the sole desire to liven up the proceedings'. Robertson-Glasgow likened him to Coeur de Lion 'knocking off some Saracen's head', with a belief in his ability to win over anyone. That was his personality. At the beginning of the tour he bet a Fremantle wharfie £1 that England would win the series. When, on the return journey, the wharfie attempted to pay, Chapman simply grinned. There was to be no-one quite like him again. The Neville Cardus tribute to C.B. Fry, in the 1957 *Wisden*, applied also to the Chapman role and style: 'he belonged . . . . to an age not obsessed by specialism; he was one of the last of the English tradition of the amateur, the connoisseur, and, in the most delightful sense of the word, the dilettante'.

Douglas Jardine was utterly different. Born an only child in 1900, independence and aloofness marked his character early. At Horris Hill, an English preparatory school with a good cricket coaching tradition, he corrected a master on a technical point by referring him to C.B. Fry's *Art of Batsmanship*. He left Winchester for New College, Oxford, as a leading England schoolboy player with a string of fine performances behind him and a glittering career ahead. In 1921 he scored 96 not out for Oxford against the Australian touring side before the match was called off early. Some writers have argued that he never forgot the incident, and that thereafter his inherent tough-mindedness became pronounced when playing against Australia. He left Oxford with a modest fourth class degree in 1923 and, while playing for Surrey, qualified as a solicitor by 1926.

Although playing little regular cricket for much of the 1920s, he was selected for the 1928–29 MCC tour and discovered Australian crowd behaviour, a phenomenon to which he was never reconciled. He led teams against India and New Zealand in 1931 and 1932 before being chosen to lead the 1932–33 team to Australia. His leadership experience was limited, but his attitude towards the game clearly impressed

Douglas Jardine

the selectors. On hearing that Jardine had been appointed captain of England Rockley Wilson, then a Winchester cricket coach who had been a 1920–21 MCC tourist in Australia, is reported to have said: 'Well, we shall win the Ashes—but we may lose a Dominion'.

Beyond the cricket field, Jardine was more complex than most, if not all, of his predecessors and successors as England captain. In his tour book *In Quest of the Ashes*, a chapter on fishing refers to his youthful tutelage by Andrew Lang. Lang died in 1912 after spending most of his life as a writer on a bewildering array of subjects: literature, anthropology, Scottish history, fishing and golf to name a few. His great fame, though, came from his compilations of fairy tales and children's stories, which grew out of his work on mythology, the supernatural and psychic phenomena. Lang was also friendly with such writers as Robert Louis Stevenson, H. Rider Haggard and A.E.W. Mason who shared interests in tradition, the Empire and the mysterious. This was the man who so influenced the young Jardine.

Jardine retained an interest in psychic matters. While at Oxford he became friendly with a young woman called Joan Marshall through his Old Wykehamist circle. In her autobiography *Time Out of Mind*, Joan Grant (as she became after marrying Leslie Grant, one of Jardine's friends) recalled Jardine as the man who daringly took her out to inspect the Lord's pitch, an unusual privilege for a woman. Grant became famous for books like *The Winged Pharoah* which recounted her lives in earlier incarnations. She moved widely amongst those interested in the psychic and the supernatural.

Perhaps Lang's influence is also shown in Jardine's love of A.A. Milne. Jardine's daughter retains her father's library which includes mint copies of every Milne work, autographed both by Milne and Ernest Shepard, his illustrator. Milne's son Christopher, archetype for Christopher Robin, writes in his *The Enchanted Places* of cricket's importance in the house, and of important cricketers. J.M. Barrie, another cricket enthusiast and creator of *Peter Pan*, fell into the circle, too—perhaps that prompted his irony-laden letter to *The Times*, at the height of the bodyline crisis, suggesting that if cricket was made only for batsmen to get big scores then the laws should certainly be altered to prevent bowlers from becoming too successful.

Later in life Jardine became interested in Hinduism developing, according to a relative's note in *The Times* on 24 June 1958, an antipathy to Christianity. He was excited by discussions of ethics and religion, especially when attacking 'Rewards and Fairies', as he called Christianity. Interestingly enough, the phrase refers to the title of a book by Rudyard Kipling, another imperial writer deeply interested in the psychic after losing a son in the First World War.

Harold Larwood came from a world vastly different to that of his captain. Born in Nuncargate, Nottinghamshire, he began working in the local coal mines at the age of fourteen. His cricket was learned initially from his father who captained the colliery side. An old English player who lived nearby thought Larwood showed promise and recommended him to the county authorities. By 1924, when he was still not twenty, Larwood had played for the county, and by 1926 he was playing for England. He toured Australia in 1928–29 and enjoyed some success, but in 1930 he suffered at the hands of Bradman as did all English bowlers that year. On his own report, however, he learned that Bradman disliked short-pitched deliveries. Between 1930 and 1932 Larwood improved his accuracy so that he could direct such an attack to a carefully placed field. Much of the bodyline controversy consequently revolved around what the Manchester *Guardian* called 'the contrast between the revolutionary and the classical idea', a clash between old and new conventions of cricket behaviour. In the five test matches Larwood bowled 220 overs (50 more than any other bowler) and took 33 wickets (Allen, with 21, was the next most successful) at an average of 19.51 runs per wicket. Of English bowlers who have toured Australia since, only Frank Tyson in 1954–55 and John Snow in 1970–71 have approached his 1932–33 record, a performance which ranks as one of the greatest fast bowling feats of all time.

Donald George Bradman, the main object of attention for Jardine and Larwood, was born the son of a carpenter in Cootamundra, New South Wales, in 1908 and later moved with his family to Bowral. He scored heavily in local cricket from the age of twelve; centuries were regular, double and triple centuries not uncommon. By the age of eighteen he had attracted the attention of the New South Wales selectors, even though he was a country player with no turf wicket experience. The selectors were impressed at a Sydney trial and, through a system of cricket patronage, he entered grade cricket there. During the 1927–28 season he played regularly for New South Wales, scoring a century on debut and finishing with an average of 46. A good performance against

Harold Larwood

the touring MCC side the following season gained him selection for the first test. Australia was ground into submission, and Bradman failed. Dropped for the second test, he was recalled for the third to make 79 and 112, then scored another century in the fifth. Another successful domestic season was followed by selection for the 1930 England tour. Then 22, Bradman turned on the most phenomenal batting feat ever seen. He scored 2960 runs in all games at an astonishing average of 98. His test record was even more spectacular: 974 runs in 7 innings at an average of 139. Even so, Australia won the series by only two matches to one with two drawn. Bradman clearly made the difference between the sides, and his success marked the real birth of bodyline as English cricket sought to nullify the genius of the 'boy from Bowral'.

Bradman became a new kind of Australian sports personality. Confounding the view that Australian cricketers were strictly amateurs, he turned sports success to commercial advantage, challenging the authority and traditional values of Australian cricket administrators. While in England he wrote *Don Dradman's Book* which was serialised in the press. When he returned to Australia the Board of Control withheld one-third of his tour bonus, and £50 was a substantial sum at the start of the economic depression. The Board argued that he had contravened a contract clause forbidding players from writing about matches in which they were involved.

This did not diminish Bradman's public popularity. Australian player and journalist Jack Fingleton recalled how Bradman left the rest of the Australian team in Perth after the 1930 tour to undertake a triumphal overland journey. Some players did not take kindly to this, arguing that Bradman's commercial commitments were so great during the tour that they only saw him when he went out to bat. This commercial image was consolidated late in 1931 when he signed a joint contract with a newspaper, a radio station and a sports goods organisation. At the beginning of the next season the Board told Bradman that he could not play and write, and for a while it seemed that he would not play against Jardine's side. That he did so suggests that cricket's new commercial aspect was a powerful one in an age of economic stress, and marked a new phase in player–authority relationships.

The English tour opened in Perth with matches against Western

Donald Bradman

Australia and an invitation team which included Bradman. He failed in both innings on a damp wicket, but there was no bodyline bowling involved. The MCC then beat South Australia and Victoria convincingly, again without short-pitched bowling. Bodyline made its first appearance in Melbourne against another invitation team. Bradman fared badly, falling to Larwood in both innings, moving away from the flying deliveries and playing them unorthodoxly. Australian captain Bill Woodfull, playing more correctly, took the first of many heavy body blows he was to receive in the following weeks. Larwood was rested for the New South Wales match, but Bradman and Jack Fingleton still looked most uncomfortable against the short-pitched bowling of left-hander Bill Voce.

The key figures did not meet in the first test on the Sydney Cricket Ground: Bradman was ruled unfit to play because of illness. The Australian innings of 360 belonged to New South Wales player, Stan McCabe, whose 187 not out remains among the most courageous of test innings. Defying the bodyline bowling and field, he hooked the rising ball with power despite the risk of being caught. South Australian Victor Richardson (whose Chappell descendants later came to dominate Australian cricket) chimed in with 49 to see Australia into at least a comfortable position. Harold Larwood took 5 wickets for 96 runs, Bill Voce, his Nottinghamshire colleague, 4 for 110, but their methods were so unpopular that a writer in the English *Observer* accused Australian journalists of inflaming public opinion. The Board of Control was to meet in Melbourne during the second test, and there were reports that the MCC Committee would be asked to impose restraints upon its team's tactics.

England replied with 524. Herbert Sutcliffe of Yorkshire, senior professional on the tour, reached his highest test match score of 194. Walter Hammond, a later England captain, made 112. The Nawab of Pataudi made 102 on his test debut, as had P.F Warner, his manager on this tour. Larwood then took 5 for 28 to dismiss Australia for 164, leaving England just one run to score for victory on the last morning of the match.

Bradman came back for the second test on the Melbourne Cricket Ground. Buoyed by their Sydney success, Jardine and his fellow selectors chose four fast bowlers and no slow bowler for the match. The decision seemed vindicated when Yorkshire's Bill Bowes dismissed Bradman on the first ball to take his only wicket in the test series, the

Australian swinging wildly at a bouncer. Bowes later recalled that the 'crowd was stupified. Bradman walked off the field amid a silence that would have been a theatrical producer's triumph.' However, the pitch was generally too slow for the English bowlers and the Australians made 228, Fingleton prising out 83.

England made just 169, Sutcliffe contributing 52. For Australia, Bill 'Tiger' O'Reilly took 5 for 63 and Tim Wall 4 for 52, but their efforts looked in vain when Australia managed only 191 in its second innings. Bradman alone kept his team in the match. His 103 not out earned him a collection from the spectators, and he later bought a piano with the proceeds.

England never looked like winning, however, as O'Reilly (5 for 66) and local man 'Dainty' Ironmonger (4 for 26) dismissed them for 139, so squaring the series if not easing the tension. Larwood was booed on numerous occasions when Australian batsmen were hit. Most of the Australian press and public were uneasy. Even the Melbourne *Argus*, a paper of sober tone, was worried, reassuring itself and its readers that 'cricket is a grand old game, no matter what may have been done to it by those who sublimate it and call the result Test cricket'.

The scene shifted to the Adelaide Oval for the third match in the series. Interest was so high that special trains carried three times the normal number of passengers from Melbourne to the South Australian capital, where the Englishmen became unpopular before the match even began. Upset by the behaviour of a youthful crowd at practice sessions, Jardine had the ground closed to spectators. The *Sydney Morning Herald* hoped that such unpleasantness would not prevent the game from being 'played in the tradition and the spirit that have made it what it is—the true embodiment of British sport and fair play'.

England batted first and made 341 after being 4 for 30 at an early stage. Leyland, Wyatt and Paynter came to the rescue. So, too, did Hedley Verity, one of the finest-ever left arm bowlers and destined to die in an Italian prisoner-of-war camp during the Second World War. Tim Wall took 5 for 72 on his home ground, only to see his side then dismissed for 222.

Australia began its innings on the Saturday afternoon before a capacity crowd and in extremely hot conditions. Woodfull was soon hit over the heart by a rising delivery from Larwood and 'vehement protests' came from the spectators. Their anger was heightened by

16

Jardine making the only move he expressed regret for, immediately switching his fieldsmen from orthodox to bodyline positions. Numerous 'hostile demonstrations' followed when other batsmen ducked under similar deliveries. Play resumed on Monday, the ground crammed by yet another record crowd which, no doubt, had absorbed during the rest day all available press and radio reports. The atmosphere, tense from the outset, erupted when Australian wicket-keeper Bert Oldfield glanced a short-pitched ball from his bat into his face. One English reporter, Bruce Harris, felt that 'if some impetuous member of the crowd had set himself up as leader any number would have followed him over the fence with unimaginable results'. Herbert Mishael, a young sportswriter on duty at the ground with the Melbourne *Age* press team, years later recalled the same feeling. Newsreel film shows sections of the crowd shaking the picket fence. Even the normally staid and socially respectable members' stand was in a tumult. There were later reports that mounted police armed with batons (some reports even said automatic weapons) had been sent to the ground for fear of an imminent full-scale disturbance. Jack Hobbs, just retired from an illustrious test career for England and now in Australia to write about the tour, left the ground worn out by the crowd noise which an Australian observer agreed was 'remarkably' hostile.

Australian crowd behaviour had bothered English touring teams for many years, mainly because Australian spectators shouted advice of all kinds to players during the course of the game. This was very different from the demure atmosphere that generally surrounded English cricket grounds, although English crowds were not always quiescent. 'Barracking', as it was known, had emerged in Australia at least as early as the 1890s, and one exponent of the art estimated that by the 1930s it was practised by at least 70 per cent of Australian cricket watchers. However, participation was almost entirely verbal, invasions of the pitch being almost unknown, and apparent ill-feeling rarely outlasted the duration of the game. One spectator in Adelaide, for example, gave vent to his anger with Jardine by shouting during a drinks break, 'Don't give *him* a drink! Let the bastard die of thirst!'

In 1932–33 there was a sharper edge to this abrasive but relatively ordered crowd participation, and it may be linked to the underlying social and economic conditions. The crowds were bigger than ever before. Record attendances were set on nearly every ground, and a world record for cricket match attendance was set during the Melbourne test. Spectators went to great lengths to be assured of a good vantage point. In Melbourne, for example, the first enthusiasts reached the gates at 5.30 on the first morning, many ate breakfast outside the ground, and an hour before the gates opened a twelve-wide queue was over a quarter of a mile long. One correspondent thought the spectators needed, more than ever before, to identify with a standard of excellence attained by a champion so that they might reassert some of their general social confidence. Larwood thought that many were at the grounds in anticipation of an Australian victory which might provide hope and encouragement in the face of unemployment and dole queues. Jack Fingleton explained much of Bradman's public popularity in similar terms; to see Bradman succeed was to see Australia triumph in the face of adversity.

It is easier to evoke the size and atmosphere of those crowds than to analyse their composition. It is unwise, for example, to assume that they were 'middle-class' simply because, given the depressed economy, it was relatively costly to attend the matches. People were *prepared* to pay to see the cricket because they thought it would offer them some degree of psychological comfort and a good deal of entertainment. One Melbourne man, though he could 'ill-afford' to do so, paid 8 shillings for two stand seats so that he might give his wife a day's entertainment. People like him paid almost £70 000 in gate takings at the five tests, and the *Argus* calculated that for admission, transport, and refreshments the Melbourne crowd spent at least £40 000 to watch the second test.

The crowds probably reflected the general social mix of Australian society. A number of observers confirmed this by drawing social distinctions between people who sat in members' stands and those who watched from the 'outer'. Important here is that both sections reacted angrily to English tactics during the really fiery moments of bodyline, particularly in Adelaide. In a time of general stress, there was a degree of social cohesion and identity perhaps unmatched in any other social situation of the time. Large numbers of people thoroughly identified with the fortunes of cricket.

With a lead of 119, then, England pressed home its advantage with a second innings total of 412. Hammond led the way with 85, and Jardine's 56 was his only half-century in the series. Bill O'Reilly again struggled to keep Australia in the match, taking 4 for 79 off a marathon

50 overs. In a tenacious display Australian captain Woodfull batted through the second innings for 73 not out, but the mentally weary and physically battered Australians could struggle to just 193. Bradman again battled audaciously for 66, while Larwood and Allen each took 4 wickets to put England ahead in the series.

In a sour atmosphere the tour proceeded to the Brisbane Cricket Ground. Richardson, Bradman and Woodfull carried Australia to 340 with Larwood taking 4 for 101 under trying conditions. In England's 356 Sutcliffe again top-scored, this time with 86, but the innings came from Lancastrian Eddie Paynter. Having taken sick during Australia's first innings, in a 'Boy's Own' performance he rose from a hospital bed to score 83 and put England ahead on the first innings.

Larwood took another 3 wickets in Australia's second innings, although already beginning to suffer from the foot injury which eventually put him out of cricket for a while. Needing just 160 to win the series England lost Sutcliffe early, but Jardine batted solidly, Maurice Leyland scored 88, and they were home. Fittingly, Paynter finished the match with a six as England ended at 4 for 162.

Australia's pride and the size of England's winning margin for the Ashes were the only issues at stake in the final Sydney test. Australia made an excellent start scoring 435: new players Darling (85) and O'Brien (61) played well, with other good scores from McCabe, Oldfield (recovered from his injury), Bradman and Lee, another new player. Larwood took another 4 wickets as Jardine persisted in his fast bowling tactics. Not to be outdone, England scored 454. Hammond reached his second century of the series, while Larwood made 98. He was sent in late one afternoon, as night watchman, survived a few overs, then set about the bowling the next morning. The Sydney crowd gave him a great ovation as he left the ground, having just missed what would have been his only test hundred.

For once, it was not the English fast bowlers who did the damage in Australia's second innings. Hedley Verity bowled tightly to take 5 for 33 as Australia fell to 182, having reached 115 before the fall of the second wicket. England then reached 2 for 168, Hammond ending the match and the series with a six.

The series averages are instructive (See Table 1). The England batting was more solid, averaging 35.8 runs per wicket against Australia's 25.4. It had more depth, two players scoring over 400 in the series while

Table 1   Leading batting and bowling averages in the 1932–33 test series

Batting

England				Australia			
Paynter	5 innings	184 runs	61.3 average	Bradman	8 innings	396 runs	56.6 average
Sutcliffe	9	440	55.0	McCabe	10	385	42.8
Hammond	9	440	55.0	Darling	4	148	37.0
Wyatt	9	327	46.7	Woodfull	10	305	33.9
Pataudi	3	122	40.6	Lee	2	57	28.5
Leyland	9	306	34.0	Richardson	10	279	28.0

Bowling

England				Australia			
Larwood	33 wickets	644 runs	19.5 average	Wall	16 wickets	409 runs	25.5 average
Mitchell	3	60	20.0	O'Reilly	27	724	26.8
Verity	11	271	24.6	Ironmonger	15	405	27.0
Voce	15	407	27.1	Lee	4	163	40.7
Allen	21	593	28.2	Bradman	1	44	44.0
Hammond	9	291	32.3	Nagel	2	110	55.0

Source: Wisden, 1934

Australia had none. Three players for England averaged over 50; only Bradman did so for Australia. This gave England an advantage, and it would have been a greater one but for Bradman. He certainly did not fail, but he was contained. The pattern was similar in bowling. England averaged a wicket every 25.4 runs, Australia every 35.8, with Larwood making the real difference. While Wall and Ironmonger bowled well, their averages were significantly higher than those of Larwood's main support bowlers. Overall, then, it should not be forgotten that England's batting was a key element in it's victory, supporting Larwood's effort in the field.

The touring party headed to New Zealand, relaxation and high scores—Hammond made 336 not out in the Auckland test to break Bradman's record set at Leeds in 1930. Then it was back home to face MCC inquiries into the circumstances surrounding the tour, and to await new developments in the war of words as opposed to the conflict between bat and ball.

A generation of cricket devotees throughout the British Empire grew up in the knowledge that the Adelaide test in January 1933 had almost ended, for a time at least, cricket relations between England and Australia. In that test, far from being one of the main cultural bridges of the Empire, cricket came closest to rending it asunder. While political and economic tensions might strain good-will in restricted circles, cricket was general currency—that was a major reason for the 1932–33 tour becoming so critical. It might be equated with the damage done to British prestige at the popular level by the supposed inefficiencies in its generals' disposition of Australian troops during the First World War.

The analogy is not so curious, because Australia developed a love-hate ambivalence toward Jardine which bore out the point. His methods and ruthless efficiency so hated in one sphere might become acceptable in another, as Ray Robinson wrote in *Between Wickets* just after the Second World War:

> Nothing the War Office did from 1939 onward puzzled Australians more than the failure to make use of D.R. Jardine's talent for generalship by setting him up alongside Field-Marshal Montgomery (who called his staff his First XI and foretold that he would hit Rommel for six out of Africa).

---

rd Inspector, describing how a number of women ransacked
ty rubbish in a city vegetable market. They had with them
babies, including twins. The correspondent found it
every clean living person' and difficult to believe that any
ld fall as low as that. Such, however, were the times in
odyline tour was played.

not all or even many of those caught up in the bodyline
were fully alive to its relationship with the pervading social
connection was rather indirectly important as grievance
ievance to produce heated argument at the most individual

cInnes, an English-born university student, recalled an
is over 30 years later in his autobiography, *Humping My*
staying with friends in Tasmania at the time, and cricket
passionately and at great length. Although McInnes
e's demeanour overly arrogant, he was still a 'Pom' in
s. As the tour developed, feelings began to run very high.
me with the Adelaide test. McInnes's friends cooled
ith some unable to bring themselves to speak. It became
hat he packed to leave, exiled by bodyline as he put it.
moment was he asked to stay on.

rectly points to another major factor to be remembered
he passions raised by bodyline—the media. Because of
rtance in Australia and England, cricket was always big
ur, it arguably became bigger news than ever because of
ts: the nature of the cricket itself and the rapidly rising
io. McInnes recalled the roar of the Adelaide crowd
in his Tasmanian lounge. Throughout the depression
s the major source of information and entertainment in
ith this tour, cricket became part of that for the first
ries were beamed across the country so that even
places were in immediate contact with events. Famous
yers were snapped up by radio stations to provide
and, in these early days before controls were
harsh words went out over the airwaves.

e, newspapers provided a volume of material. Th
highpoint was at least 30 strong, so that during th
st 140 000 words (almost three times the size of thi

Yet a few years earlier Jardine, for most Australians, had been the man who destroyed the sacred heritage of cricket. He transgressed the cardinal lore of cricket by playing within the law but outside spirit and convention. Australian cricket had a strong tradition of following spirit and convention, so to have the very envoy of cricket's ultimate authority destroy them was a shattering blow.

For many English followers, on the other hand, such protestations of principle were interpreted as another round of 'squealing' from colonial whingers who took their games far too seriously and could not bear to lose. Even when bodyline tactics appeared on English soil subsequently to considerable alarm, there was a satisfaction that Jardine was able to score his only test century against it. That is, unlike the Australians he met it, conquered it and did not squeal. By the end of the tour such feelings were deepseated and persistent. After the final resolution of the crisis, involving the demise of Larwood and the retirement of Jardine, the MCC received a number of letters lamenting what was seen as a sell-out to the colonials. One, written early in 1935, thought the English principals in the drama had been treated cowardly, especially in view of Australians' prevailing attitudes towards Britain. The correspondent claimed to have seen English migrants pelted with rubbish in Perth during the 1920s; considered that Victoria had steadfastly refused to honour its obligations towards migrants; claimed that Australia put up high tariffs, yet sought Empire Free Trade and screamed for open beef markets in Britain, all the while breaking trade agreements so placing British manufacturers in jeopardy. Under such circumstances, the MCC should not have given in. A British evangelist who had been in Brisbane for 43 years put it even more strongly: those people who let down Jardine were traitors who had betrayed the millions of Britons living in the colonies and trying to promote civilisation.

That such views were held so strongly was not due solely to cricket matters, no matter how fiery they were. Conditions in both countries, for example, provided a background of substantial tension and fragile social relations. The touring side left an England vastly different from that left by any previous team. The period from September 1932 to January 1933—which coincided almost exactly with the tour programme—marked the depths of the depression in Britain. At least 20 per cent of the workforce was unemployed, and bankruptcies rose by 12

per cent between 1930 and 1932. N
rose by over 60 per cent between 1
by unemployment, it was argued,
than usual to those who are loyal
"play the game". In Kindon
employed by local land-owners
members of the British Worker
property traditionally administer

In the midst of this widespre
reassuring for the middle classes
but the model of middle-class
going off to Australia with a
autographed for the son of L
least, retained its social stabili

When they landed at Frer
players found themselves in as
had left. At least 29 per cent o
with the figure being as high
were conservative figures, ta
non-unionists. Even those w
for the fall in real wages far
in England, there were fea
tributing to the breakdo
organiser was on trial in Sy
to join his organisation. T
the implementation of c
unemployment assistanc
necessity of a city campai
of discipline in school a

That 'failure' was man
Secretary of the South
(also Secretary to the
missioner of Police se
Oval, including the p
racking, in particular,
of increased bad langı
about the time of the

Health Boa
daily the di
very young
'repulsive t
woman sho
which the b
Of course
controversy
crisis. The
built upon g
level.

Graham M
example of th
Bluey. He was
was discussed
thought Jardi
Australian eye
The climax c
towards him, w
so unpleasant
Only at the las
McInnes ind
in considering
its cultural imp
news. On this to
two developmen
influence of rad
being broadcast
radio was perhap
Australia and, w
time. Commenta
people in remote
players or ex-pla
'expert' opinions
developed, many
At the same tin
press camp at its
Adelaide test at le

book) were sent out to all parts of the world. Gilbert Mant, the Reuter's correspondent, sent cables on the test matches to every major British colony in the world. Added to that were the press photographers and newsreel film crews whose products clearly had a dramatic impact on the public perception of bodyline. While the extent and sophistication of that coverage might now look basic, at the time it deluged Australia with the most continuous and extensive information of any sport event to that point. Along with this went information on the social and economic ills of the time, building up the indirect connection between cricket and the general condition. By the end of the bodyline crisis, then, a considerable collective consciousness had built up about it on both sides of the world. In Britain, for example, a cartoon by the famous David Low carried his predictions for the fourth test: Larwood hits Bradman on the jaw; Bradman hurls his bat at Larwood; fielders throw Bradman into the stumps; Jardine bites Woodfull; the Australian government considers an MCC cable advising that biting is part of cricket; stop press—Australia declares war. These collective views were soon solidified, first, by postmortem examinations from the British press upon the team's arrival home and, secondly, by the tour books which appeared throughout 1933.

Australian sensitivities were affronted first by reports that Larwood, intercepted by journalists on the continent before reaching England, had accused Bradman of cowardice. Larwood's book, *Body-Line?*, appeared soon after to stoke the fires:

> I am left with no alternative but to believe, that if there is a doubt that some of Australia's batsmen haven't the courage to stand up to fast bowling on a fast wicket, there is no doubt whatever that most of those who write about cricket in the Australian Press have no pluck at all.

Elsewhere Larwood referred to

> the offensive, vulgar, and outrageous behaviour of the ill-bred sections of the Australian crowds, in which I include those occupants of the higher-priced seats at the cricket grounds who, for that very reason alone, ought to know better and ought to give the lead to the cheap ring, who, in their turn, are educated by the gutter-press . . .

25

To a cricketing world more used to the measured tones of a Neville Cardus, this was strong stuff not designed to obliterate bodyline memories.

For the next few months, the bodyline generation was wearied by blast and counterblast from English and Australian authors, ranging from the sober to the sensationalist. Australian player Alan Kippax, one of the players shaken by bodyline, wrote in *Anti-Bodyline* that Larwood's views were quite unwarranted, that great publicity in England had clearly unhinged the fast bowler's judgement. As for the Australian crowds, far from being out of control their forbearance of the ugly bowling tactics was highly commendable, socially responsible and evidence of advanced nationhood. Back came Bruce Harris, tennis writer turned cricket correspondent, with *Jardine Justified: the Truth About The Ashes*:

> The Australian barracker was usually irritating, seldom impartial, often rude and offensive, and only occasionally funny. I have never seen a worse display of bad manners from any crowd than that which disgraced the barracking section of the Hill at Sydney in booing Jardine for two or three minutes during the fifth Test Match . . .

Harris's title reflected a growing concern that somewhere there was a truth, and in it lay a defence of Jardine: 'England's captain was no cricketing ogre, deaf and blind to generous instincts'. He was, according to Harris, a man of sensitivity, compassion and even humour.

Most Australians, however, saw the English captain as the destroyer of cricket. R.W.E. Wilmot put this view reasonably in *Defending The Ashes*. A sports journalist of long experience, Wilmot was educated at Melbourne Grammar and Melbourne University where the civilising influence of cricket was taken very seriously. To him, Jardine and, to a lesser extent, Warner had betrayed the spirit of cricket so important in maintaining good relations between England and Australia: 'it is easy to insist that cricket must be played by sportsmen and in a sporting spirit, that all suspicion of unfairness be removed, and that the spirit of the game be observed in all things'. Other criticisms were less restrained. One of the most remarkable, by a 'Man in the Street', was entitled *The 'Sporting' English? From Front Line to Bodyline*. The English attitude to cricket, the writer argued, was characteristic of its attitudes to Australia in general: 'The plain, unadorned truth about sport in England is that there is so much cant talked on the subject that it offers unique opportunities for hypocrisy.' This applied also to English views on Australian culture and attempts to minimise the Australian contributions to the war effort.

Works like R.T. Corrie's *The Barracker at Bay*, along with the more moderate books which appeared during 1933, were not written in a cricket vacuum, because the bodyline events put Australia's 1934 tour of England in doubt until the very last moment. Agreed rule changes took almost a year to produce, so the extension of the bodyline fire from field to page heightened rather than reduced the polarisation of national attitudes about what had happened. As a result, bodyline passed into folklore more rapidly and substantially than any other cricket event. Most Australians of the time took in a fund of stories relating English iniquities and Australian heroism. On the English side, there remained a persistent niggling doubt that the Australians 'squealed' simply because they lost.

Once the 1934 tour went ahead, with the MCC largely finding against the bodyline theory and Jardine having left cricket, discussion of the affair went into curious abeyance. It was almost as if both parties realised what a close thing to cricket ruination it had been, so agreed to pretend that it never happened—supported in the illusion by the cricket world. Gubby Allen returned to Australia as leader of the MCC in 1936–37, his Australian family connection and his enthusiasm for public speeches guaranteeing the tour's social success.

In the following 40 years, many books on cricket referred briefly to the crisis and a handful of works concentrated on the tour itself. By far the most important was Jack Fingelton's *Cricket Crisis*. The only book on the event by an Australian who played throughout the series, and written after the immediacy of it all, its skilfully and carefully measured views made it by far the best on the subject. For the rest, the facts, views and personalities were reworked, but nothing was added to a fuller understanding of the affair despite persistent rumours that bodyline *had* got off the cricket field and into the political backrooms.

Not long after the Second World War Harold Larwood and his family settled in Australia, being well-received by the public. He was asked frequently for his views on the affair and eventually had another book published which revised some of his 1933 views, but did not alter the public perception of bodyline. As for Douglas Jardine, it was widely thought that he returned to Australia for the only time in 1957 even though his business interests included Australian property. However, as revealed in a letter by him preserved in the Sir Robert Menzies papers now held in the Australian National Library, Canberra, he met the then Prime Minister at least once before 1957 in the country of his earlier exploits, in January 1954. Then, as later, he was publicly silent on bodyline. Whenever Menzies was in London for politics and cricket, though, Jardine was always a dinner guest until his death in 1958.

It took the fiftieth anniversary of the tour to create systematic re-examinations of bodyline, but the new accounts go little beyond the traditional views and seek no reinterpretation. This book does, however, and its starting point lies in the nature of cricket's imperial significance.

2
The empire of cricket

In the midst of the 1932–33 tour a British resident in Rhodesia wrote to the *Australian Cricketer*: 'You would no doubt be surprised to see how keenly cricket enthusiasts are following the progress of the MCC tour.' That simple message hints at one major yet neglected impact of the bodyline controversy—upon a previously unshakeable belief in cricket as a code of cultural behaviour throughout the British Empire.

Prince Ranjitsinjhi, England's pre-eminent example of cricket's imperial value, stated the game's position clearly in his *The Jubilee Book of Cricket*, published to mark Queen Victoria's fiftieth year as monarch in 1897. The book's final chapter was entitled 'Cricket and the Victorian Era', and it revealed the depth of contemporary feeling about cricket as a training for life. Self-control, for example, was seen as a cricket trait, for both players and spectators: 'Something that keeps 25 000 people in order without external direction or suppression must be very real'. Physical training, of course, was also very important in that cricket prepared men for military service, should it become necessary, and in a pleasurable way, unlike squad drill. Because of that enjoyment, cricket encouraged men into voluntarily realising their capabilities more easily than those trained under duress.

Ranjitsinjhi then made two points of indirect importance in understanding bodyline. First, he pointed to cricket as largely an association of ideas:

No doubt when people play the game on a rough jungle of veldt-grass and mine-tailings in the outskirts of Johannesburg, half the pleasure they find is ... the feel of a bat and its sound against the ball bring [ing] back memories of the green turf and cool breezes of England.

29

In that sense, cricket provided a bond with the mother country, a theme recurrent in cricket literature until at least the Second World War, and sometimes beyond. To think of cricket was to think of England; to play it or watch it was as if to be in England; and to accept its conventions was to behave as if in England.

Secondly, said Ranjitsinjhi, cricket 'seems to have an extraordinarily good influence both upon those who take an active part in it and upon those who are merely spectators'. The 'good influence', of course, expressed cricket's power in wide-ranging areas. Anyone who took the game seriously was 'a far better exponent of the art of living than many men who are far richer and far more highly esteemed' because work and leisure combined to produce satisfaction and contentment.

This view was all the more powerful coming from a man whose life story bore out its precepts. Ranji, as he was known, was born in India in 1872. His high-status Rajput family lived 40 miles south of Nawanagar, capital of a small princely state of the same name which was one of the many collectively known as the Kathiawar states ruled indirectly by the British through a Political Agent. The whole area fell within the boundary of the old Bombay Presidency. While Ranji was growing up, his state was a little under 4000 square miles in area, with most of its population of 300 000 living in about 600 villages. The annual land revenue was around £300 000, and the main commercial products were silk cloth, gold embroidery, dyes and perfumes.

'Ranji' might never have appeared on the international cricket field had it not been that in 1879 the childless ruler, the Jam Saheb of Nawanagar, adopted him as his heir. Because of strong political rivalries for the position within harem factions, the young Ranji was closely guarded. For his early schooling he was sent to Rajkumar College in nearby Rajkot. It was a school specially set up for the scions of ruling families so that they might imbibe the best English traditions. In their curriculum, naturally, was cricket, coached by the principal who was an old Cambridge man. Ranji spent eight years here and cricket was one of his great successes. Along with its rules and its achievements he learned its traditions and conventions of teamwork, discipline and sportsmanship. In 1889 he went to Cambridge, becoming, one of very few young Indians in English higher education at the time. His reception by cricket authorities was cool. They considered his style too adventurous and unorthodox. None the less he earned great respect for his diligent practice in the nets—after all, 'practice makes perfect' was one of the great cricket sayings. In 1892 he went to Trinity College and played for its team but missed out on a University place, even though he might have been good enough. There was little thought then of an Indian playing for Cambridge in the most aristocratic of games. Despite a wretched performance in the 1893 Oxford–Cambridge match, his other performances that year gained him wide recognition and by the following season he had become an idol of English crowds.

During this early period, Ranji encountered many of the English cricket authorities whose strong beliefs were to have such an influence on the bodyline events. At Cambridge he was awarded his blue by Stanley Jackson, MCC Committee member and political figure by 1932–33. Jackson first saw the Indian star while touring the subcontinent as a member of Lord Hawke's side, and initially thought his style eccentric. On that same tour went Christopher Heseltine, who played in a number of Hawke's teams and was another MCC Committee member during bodyline. Plum Warner (1932–33 manager) and H.D.G. Leveson-Gower (Committee member) also played on Hawke tours which all had strong imperial overtones.

Viewed in statistical terms, Ranji's cricket career was certainly impressive. His first-class career began in 1895 and effectively concluded in 1905, even though he played the odd game right up until 1920. He scored over 24 000 runs at an average of 56 per innings, and compiled 72 centuries. In a limited test career he scored two centuries, both against Australia, including one on his debut at Manchester in 1896. He was the leading batsman in 1896 and 1900. In 1900 he scored five double centuries; in 1902 he scored three, including his highest score of 285 not out. This was cricket's 'Golden Age', full of the greatest batting talent England has ever known and Ranji, an Indian, was one of its greatest sensations.

Nowadays, when English county cricket is dominated by Pakistanis and West Indians from the erstwhile colonial Empire, it is difficult to imagine the extent of the impact Ranji had on English cricket and society. Here was an Indian playing with and overshadowing the best England had to offer. Most English people had never seen in Indian, and had been led to believe that their colonial subjects were weak, effete and incapable of achievement. Yet when they flocked to the grounds, they saw one who could sustain long innings in the face of hostile bowling attacks, then go into the field to take marvellous catches. Given cricket's role as a training for life, there was little doubt about Ranji's ability to succeed there as well.

Importantly, the crowds and Ranji's colleagues saw that he had learned more than the mere accumulation of runs. His outlook showed that he was essentially an English gentleman. Gilbert Jessop, himself a great star of the 'Golden Age', called Ranji 'a great sportsman'. His abilities, Jessop argued, combined with his sportsmanship and his personal character helped to carry cricket to the pinnacle of its development. Ranji was effectively India on trial, and he demonstrated to the British public that Indians were capable of absorbing the qualities their imperial overseers thought appropriate. Moreover, it revealed the beneficial effects of cricket as an agent of imperialism's civilising mission.

It was against this powerful background of cricket as a training for life and order that Ranji passed to his next test, that as the ruling Jam Saheb of Nawanagar. He had to prove to Indian and Briton alike that cricket *did* prepare a man for public service. Again he proved equal to the task. Nawanagar, according to popular opinion, was a backward and benighted place. Ranji set out on a vigorous modernisation plan. His greatest priorities lay in irrigation and communications. Both areas received approval from the British authorities who were keen on modern princes being 'improvers'. Ranji's efforts to promote irrigation facilities to overcome his state's severe droughts were particularly well thought of. So, too, were his educational objectives. As befitted a man of his background and achievements, he accepted the British faith in the power of education as a civilising and improving force. Whenever he entertained visiting viceroys, governors or parliamentarians, he was always at pains to show just what a modern Indian prince could do.

It would not be true to say that all his efforts were condoned by the authorities or the British public. There were frequent complaints that his budgets did not balance and, occasionally, there were direct interventions by officialdom. There was a long-standing feud with the Bombay government concerning customs dues at the state's main port, a dispute which was settled only after Ranji's death. There were hints that Ranji spent too much of his time out of India, fishing on his Irish estate or entertaining friends in England. At one point in the 1920s sections of the British socialist press ran stories about oppression in Nawanagar. But, by and large, Ranji's public work blunted all these criticisms. During the First World War he worked on recruiting campaigns and raised patriotic funds in both India and England. The last known photograph of W.G. Grace shows the 'Grand Old Man' with Ranji and A.C. MacLaren, another of the 'Golden Age', both in uniform, just after Grace had called on cricketers to make their contribution to the war.

After the war, Ranji was one of four ruling princes to work on the Montagu-Chelmsford reforms scheme which transferred some political power to the Indians. He was then chosen as one of India's three representatives to the League of Nations, a post which he filled for two years. According to C.B. Fry, who was his secretary in Geneva, Ranji's impact on society was matched only by that of the eminent Polish pianist-statesman, Paderewski. Ranji set out to impress India on the minds of all with whom he came in contact. For the remainder of his life he worked for the interests of the Chamber of Princes. Late in the 1920s he worked on the States Inquiry Committee, part of a wide-ranging review of British Indian political conditions; then in the 1930s he was involved with the Round Table Conferences which negotiated further political reforms.

Ranji and Lord Chelmsford, Viceroy of India 1916–21 (one-time player for Oxford and Middlesex, and MCC President in 1922) both died on the day of the 1933 Oxford–Cambridge boat race. *The Times* mourned their passing:

> A whole world of race and custom separated them, but today two nations hold them in the same memory of good sportsmanship. Ranji's name is still charged with a magic it will not lose as the greatest of English games brings men together in the most satisfying of associations. Indeed it may be against this background of a common interest, removed from all questions of political controversy, that the characters and achievements of Maharajah and ex-Viceroy are best remembered together this morning.

This obituary underlines the importance which the British attached to sport in spreading their cultural patterns, standards and conventions throughout the colonial Empire. The 'new imperialism' of the later nineteenth century coincided with the 'game revolution' which swept Britain. Administrators spread out all over the world, imbued with the athletic ideals of the great public schools and universities, and the idea that such such values could do much to consolidate British power and influence. Two particular aspects of this relationship between imperialism, education and cricket had consequences for bodyline: the power of the game's cultural hold throughout the Empire, even as late as the 1930s; and its overriding emphasis on the need for promoting and sustaining proper behaviour.

By 1932–33 England had established official cricket relationships, in the form of test matches, with all major countries in its Empire. England–Australia encounters began in 1876–77, with the MCC taking official charge of England touring teams in 1903–04. South Africa gained official status in 1888–89, the West Indies in 1928, New Zealand in 1929–30, and India in 1932. Intra-colonial games began in 1902–03 with Australia and South Africa, Australia–West Indies began in 1930–31, and South Africa–New Zealand in 1931–32.

Bodyline, in this context, came at a critical time. Cricket had just reached a high point as a form of colonial consolidation, and there was a widespread and popular belief in its power as a bonding agent for the Empire. Such a role had been sought since its early colonial introduction, and received powerful expression in Lord Hawke's Introduction to *Imperial Cricket*, edited by Pelham Warner just prior to the First World War:

> The greatest game in the world is played wherever the Union Jack is unfurled, and it has no small place in cementing the ties that bond together every part of the Empire . . . On the cricket grounds of the Empire is fostered the spirit of never knowing when you are beaten, of playing for your side and not for yourself, and of never giving up a game as lost. This is as invaluable in Imperial matters as cricket . . . the future of cricket and of the Empire . . . is so inseparably connected.

Such views were not held by the imperial masters alone. In 1927, for example, Alan Mulgan's *Home: a New Zealander's Adventure* included two chapters on cricket. These were specially revealing, given that Mulgan was one of his country's earliest writers to search for a New Zealand identity. Although he had some critical things to say about the class nature of English cricket he thought, too, that England's test victory over Australia was imperially a good thing in the middle of the 1920s:

> It showed the colonial that the Englishman could conquer on the cricket field and conquer decisively; and one must think of this test as more than a mere game, as a struggle that involved English prestige and riveted the attention of the whole Empire. In England the victory came as a bracing wind after many days of weariness. The inferiority complex had touched other things beside cricket; one feared, indeed, that it was beginning to infect national life. Then a wind blew from the Oval, and the Englishman straightened himself and said that England was not such a bad country after all.

This was a powerful metaphor, cricket as imperial life and power, which Ranji would have well understood. On the eve of bodyline, such symbolic canons could not be underestimated.

The West Indian cricket story conveyed a similar message. Unofficial tours of the islands from England began in the 1890s with one of the earliest, led by Lord Hawke, including Pelham Warner. From the beginning, cricket was a test of colonial progress and a reinforcement of imperial standard, as Hawke's comments reveal. He was keenly aware of his descent from the Admiral Hawke whose victory over the French at Quiberon Bay was commemorated by naval strategist Admiral Mahan and poet Sir Henry Newbolt. That heritage of imperial prestige was turned to cricket, and not only by the tourists, as Hawke himself recalled spectacularly:

> Ollivierre, a man of colour, shot my middle stump into the air before I had scored. He was so beside himself with joy that he promptly turned a somersault on the pitch, and then both umpires and players enthusiastically shook hands with him. Some of the crowd lost their heads with delight, beating the ground with their sticks, yelling, throwing their hats in the air and embracing each other out of sheer satisfaction.

When return visits to England began early in the new century, the tutelage tradition continued both in cricket and behavioural standards. In 1900, for example, a black fast bowler on tour sought permission to play without boots in order to improve his footing. 'Certainly not, my good man', replied his white captain, 'this is England and a first-class county to boot, sir'. By the time of the first official tour, in the words of one West Indian writer, 'the Marylebone Cricket Club, in the manner of a discerning schoolmaster, deemed the student had developed sufficiently and was ready for graduation to the highest class'. That theme of colonial grooming underlay a cartoon of the tour which had a black player declaring, 'We have come to learn, Sah'.

C.L.R. James in *Beyond A Boundary*, perhaps the most remarkable book ever written about cricket, emphasised the influence of the game on West Indian culture. Having worked his way through the colonial system by way of educational scholarships, James at an early age began demanding political independence for his islands. He became a Marxist and went to England where for many years he was active in left-wing political organisations. Yet for all that he still remained tied to the imperial system by two cultural strings—English literature and cricket. The book examines the dilemma of reconciling political radicalism with cricket's conservative ideals and how both the institutions infused West Indian life, culture and behaviour. Cricket, then, was far more than a game in its West Indian setting. It was a major cultural institution through which the imperial power bound its Caribbean colonies to itself.

In India, the jewel in the crown of Empire, the story was similar. Given an impetus in Bombay by Governor Lord Harris, cricket became a focal point for those sections of the community keen to meet the approval of the imperial masters. As in the West Indies, cricket and the English language were for many the major keys to success in a colonial system. Harris, among other governors and officials, saw a great need to capitalise upon this and said so in terms which still prevailed at the time of bodyline: 'Unquestionably interchange of visits between the Old Country and the Dominions, Dependencies, and Colonies is eminently desirable, and good conduct and good temper are productive of sympathy, and of a tightening up of the ties which hold us together.' The rhetoric of cricket in all its locations was loaded with this imperial cultural message.

Australia was no different. In the middle of the 1920s Eric P. Barbour produced *The Making Of A Cricketer*, a guide to young players. Barbour was the son of a Sydney Grammar classics teacher and cricketer, played for New South Wales before the First World War,

Australia had none. Three players for England averaged over 50; only Bradman did so for Australia. This gave England an advantage, and it would have been a greater one but for Bradman. He certainly did not fail, but he was contained. The pattern was similar in bowling. England averaged a wicket every 25.4 runs, Australia every 35.8, with Larwood making the real difference. While Wall and Ironmonger bowled well, their averages were significantly higher than those of Larwood's main support bowlers. Overall, then, it should not be forgotten that England's batting was a key element in it's victory, supporting Larwood's effort in the field.

The touring party headed to New Zealand, relaxation and high scores—Hammond made 336 not out in the Auckland test to break Bradman's record set at Leeds in 1930. Then it was back home to face MCC inquiries into the circumstances surrounding the tour, and to await new developments in the war of words as opposed to the conflict between bat and ball.

A generation of cricket devotees throughout the British Empire grew up in the knowledge that the Adelaide test in January 1933 had almost ended, for a time at least, cricket relations between England and Australia. In that test, far from being one of the main cultural bridges of the Empire, cricket came closest to rending it asunder. While political and economic tensions might strain good-will in restricted circles, cricket was general currency—that was a major reason for the 1932–33 tour becoming so critical. It might be equated with the damage done to British prestige at the popular level by the supposed inefficiencies in its generals' disposition of Australian troops during the First World War.

The analogy is not so curious, because Australia developed a love-hate ambivalence toward Jardine which bore out the point. His methods and ruthless efficiency so hated in one sphere might become acceptable in another, as Ray Robinson wrote in *Between Wickets* just after the Second World War:

Nothing the War Office did from 1939 onward puzzled Australians more than the failure to make use of D.R. Jardine's talent for generalship by setting him up alongside Field-Marshal Montgomery (who called his staff his First XI and foretold that he would hit Rommel for six out of Africa).

21

Yet a few years earlier Jardine, for most Australians, had been the man who destroyed the sacred heritage of cricket. He transgressed the cardinal lore of cricket by playing within the law but outside spirit and convention. Australian cricket had a strong tradition of following spirit and convention, so to have the very envoy of cricket's ultimate authority destroy them was a shattering blow.

For many English followers, on the other hand, such protestations of principle were interpreted as another round of 'squealing' from colonial whingers who took their games far too seriously and could not bear to lose. Even when bodyline tactics appeared on English soil subsequently to considerable alarm, there was a satisfaction that Jardine was able to score his only test century against it. That is, unlike the Australians he met it, conquered it and did not squeal. By the end of the tour such feelings were deepseated and persistent. After the final resolution of the crisis, involving the demise of Larwood and the retirement of Jardine, the MCC received a number of letters lamenting what was seen as a sell-out to the colonials. One, written early in 1935, thought the English principals in the drama had been treated cowardly, especially in view of Australians' prevailing attitudes towards Britain. The correspondent claimed to have seen English migrants pelted with rubbish in Perth during the 1920s; considered that Victoria had steadfastly refused to honour its obligations towards migrants; claimed that Australia put up high tariffs, yet sought Empire Free Trade and screamed for open beef markets in Britain, all the while breaking trade agreements so placing British manufacturers in jeopardy. Under such circumstances, the MCC should not have given in. A British evangelist who had been in Brisbane for 43 years put it even more strongly: those people who let down Jardine were traitors who had betrayed the millions of Britons living in the colonies and trying to promote civilisation.

That such views were held so strongly was not due solely to cricket matters, no matter how fiery they were. Conditions in both countries, for example, provided a background of substantial tension and fragile social relations. The touring side left an England vastly different from that left by any previous team. The period from September 1932 to January 1933—which coincided almost exactly with the tour programme—marked the depths of the depression in Britain. At least 20 per cent of the workforce was unemployed, and bankruptcies rose by 12 per cent between 1930 and 1932. Non-violent crimes against property rose by over 60 per cent between 1930 and 1933. Thieves were created by unemployment, it was argued, and constituted 'a greater menace than usual to those who are loyal to the laws of social fellowship and "play the game"'. On Kinder Scout in Derbyshire gamekeepers employed by local land-owners clashed with ramblers who were members of the British Workers' Sports Federation who walked on property traditionally administered as part of private country estates.

In the midst of this widespread social tension and change, it was reassuring for the middle classes to see Herbert Sutcliffe, a professional but the model of middle-class respectability created through cricket, going off to Australia with a cricket bat which he promised to get autographed for the son of Lord Harewood of Yorkshire. Cricket, at least, retained its social stability and ordered hierarchy.

When they landed at Fremantle in Western Australia, the MCC players found themselves in as socially fragile a situation as the one they had left. At least 29 per cent of the national workforce was unemployed, with the figure being as high as 34 per cent in some states—and those were conservative figures, taking no account of unemployment amongst non-unionists. Even those who were employed were feeling the pinch, for the fall in real wages far outstripped the decline in retail prices. As in England, there were fears that this economic dislocation was contributing to the breakdown of social order. A Communist Party organiser was on trial in Sydney for having incited unemployed workers to join his organisation. There were riots in New South Wales following the implementation of compulsory questionnaires for those seeking unemployment assistance. The *West Australian* lamented that the necessity of a city campaign against vandalism demonstrated 'the failure of discipline in school and home'.

That 'failure' was manifest everywhere. Just before the tour began the Secretary of the South Australian Cricket Association, W.H. Jeanes (also Secretary to the Australian Board) wrote to the local Commissioner of Police seeking a more diligent control of crowds at the Oval, including the placement of more plain clothes policemen. Barracking, in particular, was in need of greater control, especially because of increased bad language towards umpires and players. The poverty at about the time of the Adelaide test was conveyed in a letter to the local

23

Health Board Inspector, describing how a number of women ransacked daily the dirty rubbish in a city vegetable market. They had with them very young babies, including twins. The correspondent found it 'repulsive to every clean living person' and difficult to believe that any woman should fall as low as that. Such, however, were the times in which the bodyline tour was played.

Of course, not all or even many of those caught up in the bodyline controversy were fully alive to its relationship with the pervading social crisis. The connection was rather indirectly important as grievance built upon grievance to produce heated argument at the most individual level.

Graham McInnes, an English-born university student, recalled an example of this over 30 years later in his autobiography, *Humping My Bluey*. He was staying with friends in Tasmania at the time, and cricket was discussed passionately and at great length. Although McInnes thought Jardine's demeanour overly arrogant, he was still a 'Pom' in Australian eyes. As the tour developed, feelings began to run very high. The climax came with the Adelaide test. McInnes's friends cooled towards him, with some unable to bring themselves to speak. It became so unpleasant that he packed to leave, exiled by bodyline as he put it. Only at the last moment was he asked to stay on.

McInnes indirectly points to another major factor to be remembered in considering the passions raised by bodyline—the media. Because of its cultural importance in Australia and England, cricket was always big news. On this tour, it arguably became bigger news than ever because of two developments: the nature of the cricket itself and the rapidly rising influence of radio. McInnes recalled the roar of the Adelaide crowd being broadcast in his Tasmanian lounge. Throughout the depression radio was perhaps the major source of information and entertainment in Australia and, with this tour, cricket became part of that for the first time. Commentaries were beamed across the country so that even people in remote places were in immediate contact with events. Famous players or ex-players were snapped up by radio stations to provide 'expert' opinions and, in these early days before controls were developed, many harsh words went out over the airwaves.

At the same time, newspapers provided a volume of material. The press camp at its highpoint was at least 30 strong, so that during the Adelaide test at least 140 000 words (almost three times the size of this graduated as a medical practitioner, became active in cricket administration, and was the *Sydney Morning Herald* cricket correspondent for much of the interwar period. His philosophical views on cricket reveal the power of the imperial ethos in the Australian game at the time of bodyline. Cricket encouraged cleanness of mind and thought, and was a vital antidote to idleness induced by unemployment. As a team game it taught individual unselfishness in the collective interests of the community. It taught discipline, and moral and physical self-control. Above all, 'the regular arrangement of Test matches promotes, not only a healthy feeling of rivalry, but what is more important, a healthy feeling of friendship and unity between the Dominions and the Mother Country'.

The significance of this view cannot be stressed enough. Cricket had as powerful a hold in Australia as it did elsewhere in the Empire, and was at a height in the interwar period as political and economic changes in the imperial relationship rendered cultural ties even more important than previously. This was the culmination of a process begun in the nineteenth century. By the turn of the century, success over England at cricket was widely interpreted in Australia as the mark of a thriving society with a national independence healthily connected to a British heritage.

Major Philip Trevor, manager of the 1907–08 MCC touring side to Australia, wrote in his account of that series:

> The cricket field takes its tone, customs and feelings from the tone, customs and feelings of the greater field surrounding it. In Australia, it is admitted that there is ever a fear of dictatorship, a dislike of privilege, and even a certain repugnance to discipline. All over the world democracy's idea of a leader is a person who is to be pushed from behind and pulled back when necessary.

The underlying message is that, despite superficial differences, the core to English and Australian attitudes was the same in social and political terms.

In his account of the 1924–25 English tour Monty Noble, a distinguished Australian test player prior to the First World War, wrote of cricket as

> primarily a means of forming a character, national as well as

personal character, and if . . . we can convert these representative individuals into something in the nature of Empire-builders, we must make them of greater value to the nation and thus foster the dominant spirit that lies behind all good and all clean sport.

The concern was as much with 'clean' life and imperial relations as with sport. Noble confirmed these views when writing about Chapman's 1928–29 tour. Australia was essentially British in character but

so isolated from the motherland that we need the stimulus of regular visits from chosen ambassadors . . . and no ambassador, unless it be our governors, has greater influence for good or ill than the captain of an English eleven . . . for we can be influenced through our 'cricket sense' perhaps more easily than in any other way.

In 1930 Sir Frederick Toone, three-time MCC manager in Australia, echoed Noble's thoughts upon the wider significance of England-Australia series in a *Wisden* article:

I have from the very outset regarded these tours primarily as imperial enterprises, tending to cement friendship between the Mother Country and her Dominions. Players. . .should not be chosen for their cricket qualities alone. They must be men of good character, high principle, easy of address, and in every personal sense worthy of representing their country in all circumstances, irrespective of their work on the field.

Such attitudes were shared widely in Australia.

It occasioned no surprise, then, when at the first official welcome to Jardine's side, in Western Australia, a local politician declared:

We look upon these visits as a powerful influence in cementing the bonds of Empire. In that respect they are, I think, second only to the influence of Australian soldiers in the Great War. Australia is part of the British Empire, and its people are of the same stock as those of England.

The speaker and his generation had been raised with a reverence for cricket as far more than a mere game. Nor was it just a metaphor for life, though that would have been powerful enough—cricket was both a yardstick of and an influence upon imperial relationships. It was the bond of Empire.

At the heart of this bond lay a common code of behaviour, both on and off the field, though in practice Australia developed some different traditions. Virtually from the beginning of test matches Australian crowds indulged in what became known as 'barracking', keeping up a constant stream of advice to players, officials and anyone else in earshot. It was quite unlike the demure demeanour of English crowds, and unsettled many touring players.

Lord Harris was among the first to suffer Australian crowd behaviour during his 1879 tour when spectators at the New South Wales game rushed on to the field protesting against an umpire's decision. Harris himself suffered a blow in the midst of the mêlée, and returned to England with a dim view of colonial cricketing etiquette. Ranji himself visited Australia with Andrew Stoddart's team in 1897–98, scoring 175 in the Sydney test and noting that the crowd's unruly barracking simply had to be put up with.

When the MCC returned to Australia in 1903–04 (the first *official* MCC tour), it was led by Pelham Francis Warner, later the 1932–33 manager and later still knighted for his services to cricket. Warner was a determined rather than gifted player. He was also tactful, charming, optimistic, gently spoken and neatly dressed. In 28 test match innings he made 622 runs, one century (132 not out) and three half-centuries at an average of 23.92. He took three catches in 15 tests. But he was always regarded as a great captain with vast experience for Middlesex, and he was seen as a socially gifted touring captain — he never captained a series at home.

Warner's family background reflected the spread of the British Empire. He was born in Trinidad in 1873 (the youngest of eighteen children!) just as English cricket was moving into its imperial civilising phase. His father was Attorney-General in Trinidad for many years and one grandfather had been a magistrate there. Warner went to Barbados in 1884 to attend Harrison College, one of those colonial institutions like Ranji's Rajkumar College which produced a string of scholar-sportsmen-administrators. In 1887 after his father's death he returned to England, attending Rugby (unable to gain entry to Winchester) then Oriel College, Oxford. In 1896 he completed bar finals then set off on the first of numerous cricket tours, appropriately enough back to the

Pelham Warner

West Indies under Hawke where Trinidad was led by his brother Aucher, an earlier Oriel man who returned to cocoa estate work on the island. Hawke and Warner shared strong views about the important imperial role played by cricket.

During his 1903–04 tour, Warner was disturbed by the unseemly behaviour of all sections of Australian crowds. In Ballarat, for example, some boys were very rowdy during a minor match, and the England captain thought they should be caned to prevent them growing into barrackers such as those who disgraced the Sydney crowd. In Sydney, a run-out decision sparked a demonstration which prompted Warner to fetch Monty Noble, the opposing captain, from the pavilion. Both sat down in the middle of the ground, threatening to halt the game if the noise was not stopped.

Many English players and officials put this lack of decorum down to the over-zealous Australian approach to the game. Major Philip Trevor, manager of the 1907–08 England team in Australia, thought that, although the barrackers were a minority, Australian cricket devotees were not taught the skills of reticence so prized in England by those brought up in imperialism's cultural mainstream, like Warner.

Douglas Jardine also had a solid imperial background. His grandfather had been a barrister in India, reaching the bench in the Allahabad High Court in the United Provinces immediately after the Indian Mutiny. Two other Jardines held important legal posts in Bombay, one becoming a Judge in the High Court and the other Dean of Law in the University of Bombay. Malcolm Robert Jardine, Douglas's father, was born in 1869 and educated first at Fettes College in Edinburgh, an institution set up in 1836 on the model of the great English schools, and designed to serve the educational needs of the professional middle classes. It had an excellent reputation for games. M.R. Jardine then went on to Balliol College, Oxford, where he graduated before being admitted to the bar in 1893. He was one of the leading amateur batsmen in an age of talent, who captained Oxford then played for Middlesex. In 1894 he returned to Bombay where he was a leading supporter of cricket. He worked at the bar as well as holding a chair of law in the university, and concluded his Indian career as Advocate-General of the Bombay Presidency just as Gandhi and other nationalists began their long struggle for political independence. All the while his brother, William Ellis Jardine, carved out a very successful career in the Indian civil service arm. Thus Douglas Jardine was brought up in the strongest

The Englishmen are again finding the great Australian barracker a source of annoyance—why not pay the bloke on the hill back with some of his own medicine!

Counter measures
A cartoon by Tom Glover from Owzat *(1932)*

cricket-and-Empire tradition. His father was a contemporary of Warner, Jackson, Harris, Hawke and many others who viewed cricket as the touchstone to service of the Empire.

Jardine's dislike of Australian crowds, not to mention players, sprang from this deepseated imperial heritage. During his first Australian tour in 1928–29, his displeasure of local crowd behaviour deepened, while his position on the 1932–33 crowd reception was summed up in a chapter of his tour book. He found the crowd advice neither funny nor responsible. The Australian cricket authorities, he thought, consistently avoided their obligations to educate crowds towards better behaviour. Barracking was always unreasonable, with too many feeble excuses, and the practice undermined cricket's imperial role. Jardine recalled one state match where a dignitary being introduced to the teams was booed by the crowd, even though the visit was very important in cricket's wider social function. Here, said Jardine, 'was Democracy arrogating to itself the right to demand its full pound of flesh'. English players, he wrote, saw themselves as representatives of the mother-land, but Australian reactions rubbed off that gloss. The English players had experienced cricket in all parts of the Empire, but only in Australia was the behaviour so poor.

Among Jardine's amateurs Freddy Brown, the baby of the tour, also represented the far-flung empire of cricket. He was born in Lima, Peru, in 1910, his father being in the import-export trade there, part of Britain's strong commercial interests in South America since the later nineteenth century. His father had played league cricket around Liverpool before going to South America. When Warner took a side (including G.O. Allen) to South America in 1926–27, Brown senior took 5 for 50 against the tourists but failed to prevent a massive defeat. After a year's schooling in Valparaiso, Freddy Brown went to St Pirans and The Leys before going to Cambridge University, where he was a contempoary of G.C. Grant who went on to captain the West Indies.

G.O. 'Gubby' Allen represented a different but equally powerful strand in the intricate imperial network. His great-grandfather was born in London and arrived in New South Wales in 1816. He then became the first solicitor admitted to the local bar from the colony itself. He became Mayor of Sydney in 1845 and entered the Legislative Council in 1856. The legal firm which he founded is now the oldest in Sydney. George Wigram Allen, Gubby's grandfather, also trained for the law, becoming a magistrate and mayor of Glebe in Sydney. Active in educational circles, he entered parliament to become Minister for Justice then Speaker. He was knighted for his services, extremely wealthy (leaving an estate of £300 000 at his death in 1885), and well-connected in the Sydney social circles which placed a premium upon things British—law, literature, standards and cricket.

Gubby's father, Walter Macarthur Allen, went straight to Trinity, Cambridge, for a law degree and admission to the English bar in 1896. He married the daughter of a Queensland Minister for Lands, and began work with London's Metropolitan Special Constabulary. After some key work in supplies during the First World War he became Commander in Chief of the Metropolitan Special Constabulary, a post which he held until his death in 1943 and for which he was knighted. Gubby himself was born in Australia, educated in England, at Eton then Trinity, Cambridge. After going into commerce for a while he settled in the stock exchange. When he came to Australia for the bodyline tour, he had direct contact with a wide circle of friends and relatives, many of them influentially placed and imbued with the idea of Empire.

The Nawab of Pataudi continued the England-India connection begun by Ranji. Born the heir to a small North Indian state, he was educated in Lahore before going on to Oxford where he became one of the great university players, scoring 238 not out in the 1931 match against Cambridge. At 22 he was selected in Jardine's side after some initial doubts about his residential eligibility. Like Ranji before him, he was regarded as a great product of the imperial system. He was joined in this by his contemporary, K.S. Duleepsinjhi, Ranji's nephew, who went to school at Cheltenham in England before going to Cambridge. He played for England between 1929 and 1931, scoring 173 at Lord's in his first match against Australia. His cricket career was cut short by illness (he was selected for the bodyline tour but could not take his place) but his other work for India was crowned, appropriately enough, by his appointment as Indian High Commissioner to Australia in 1950.

The relationship between imperialism and cricket was not sustained by the administrators and amateurs alone—the professionals also took it seriously. On the 1932–33 tour Herbert Sutcliffe was senior professional and carried out his responsibility to the letter. After the 1928–29 tour he thought Jardine 'a queer fish', but by 1932–33 respected him utterly and did much to hold other players to the same line. Sutcliffe paid close attention to the cultural aspects of cricket,

44

England expects
Tom Glover's view of the England players from Owzat *(1932)*

always being neatly dressed, well-groomed and attentive to the traditions. It is even said that he strived for years to soften his Yorkshire accent so that he might be socially more acceptable in official circles. For Sutcliffe cricket provided far more than a living—it was a way of life. It is not surprising, then, that he always took his touring seriously, keen not to just play but to tighten the imperial links and substantiate his own allegiance to the system.

The English way of cricket was the best, and in that view Sutcliffe was joined by his famous opening partner, Jack Hobbs. On the 1932–33 tour Hobbs was a correspondent, complete with 'ghost' writer, for the London *Star* and *News Chronicle*. His first tour of Australia was with Philip Trevor as manager. After his second tour he wrote worriedly: 'What would strike a stranger more than anything else about the Colonial game is the very business-like manner in which it is played. In the opinion of many, it is just a little too serious.'

Hobbs and Sutcliffe certainly saw touring as financially lucrative, but they also saw it as important in maintaining British cultural superiority. After one visit to India, Sutcliffe reported to the MCC: 'We had quite a successful tour—not once were we defeated'. During that tour he appeared at Madras in the midst of political agitation, and some observers thought he helped defuse the situation. When selected to play against New Zealand in 1931 after a defeat by Australia the previous year, Sutcliffe wrote: 'May we give them a thorough trouncing in order to restore our lost prestige'. This Yorkshire-learned approach certainly endeared Sutcliffe to Jardine who, despite his university and southern England connections, loved the northern approach to the game. During the bodyline tour, the England captain could never rely so thoroughly on his other principal professional, Walter Hammond.

Hammond, one of the modern period's great batsmen, was a key to the success of the tour. Although he did not repeat his great success of 1928–29 when he scored 905 runs to average 113.1, his steadiness certainly backed Larwood's industry. But as a senior professional he was never in the same role as Sutcliffe, and his ideas on bodyline fluctuated with the situation so that Jardine never placed enormous trust in him.

Walter Hammond was born in England but taken to Malta at an early age because his father was a member of the armed services. Cricket had a strong tradition in the imperial military forces. Ranji was just one of many to see military value in the preparation given to young men by the game, and many young crickets lost their lives during the First World War. Rupert Brooke, for example, although better known as a poet, had played for Rugby school and topped the averages. Australia's Tibby Cotter was also mourned. Although the 'games' approach to war which marked 1914 and 1915 soon gave way to bitterness and regret, by 1918 there was still a belief in cricket's contribution. It was symbolic that the Australian Imperial Forces' team began postwar cricket relations with an English tour.

Cricket, then, was a powerful cultural force throughout the Empire as Jardine's side prepared to meet that of Woodfull—first in its very language, secondly in the network of personnel established throughout the Empire. Players and officials alike placed much store in the importance of those personal contacts and what they represented. Although differences in English and Australian cricketing traditions did exist, the unstated rule was to play those down at the expense of the ties that bound. Any disturbance of that status quo, then, was bound to be accepted unwillingly.

The strength of feeling on this showed up in the relief that emerged throughout the Empire when the bodyline controversy was settled without irreparable damage. There was a widespread realisation that a major link in the Empire had been nearly destroyed. Appropriately, and surely not coincidentally, the major declaration came from an Australian. When the MCC dinner to celebrate the club's 150th anniversary was held in 1937 Stanley Melbourne Bruce, Australian High Commissioner, proposed the main toast:

the MCC has a prestige and authority that is quite unrivalled. Its position in the world of cricket offers an interesting parallel to that of Great Britain in the British Empire. In theory we, the great self-governing Dominions, are autonomous communities within the British Empire, equal in status etc. In fact, we all recognise that the mother country is responsible for our existence. She has nurtured, guided and protected us throughout our history. She is a sure and certain shield and buckler for us in time of trouble and difficulty.

That such a speech could be made after the bodyline trials was an ironic tribute to the imperial power of cricket which those very trials had threatened to undermine.

3
A rift in Anglo-Australian relations

In September 1932 as Jardine and his team departed for Australia, they left behind a country seething with discontent over the high levels of unemployment. A National government composed of members of the three main political parties had been formed in August 1931, with Ramsay MacDonald the former Labour Party leader as Prime Minister. On 10 September an emergency budget was rushed through parliament. Income tax was raised as was indirect taxation collected via levies on beer, tobacco, petrol and entertainment. Unemployment benefit was cut by 10 per cent, teachers' salaries reduced by 15 per cent and smaller deductions made in the pay of the police and armed forces.

The mutiny in the Atlantic naval fleet at Invergordon happened as a direct consequences of the budget measures. The ratings staged a revolt and refused to take the ships to sea; a number of concessions were made at once but later followed by the arrest of the 'ringleaders'.

Throughout 1932 three million people were on the dole and by 1933 more than 1.5 million were receiving poor relief. Strikes disrupted the economy, one of the most bitter being the Lancashire weavers' strike in the summer of 1932 when the employers tried to impose wage reductions of between 6 and 12 per cent. Many northern towns were dominated by textile manufacturing and it appeared as if the entire community was pitched against the mill owners. Confrontations with the police became an everyday occurrence during the dispute. Despite this unrest in October 1932 the National government called a general election and gained a resounding victory. Although MacDonald remained as Prime Minister, it was Baldwin, the leader of the Conservative Party, who was the most important and influential figure in British politics.

The campaign against unemployment, organised by the National Unemployed Workers Movement, reached its height in the autumn and winter of 1932. Violent clashes between demonstrators and the police became commonplace. *The Times* described one such conflict in Liverpool in September:

> During what amounted to a series of pitched battles between the mob and the police nine officers and seven other persons were taken to hospital . . . The police tried to break up the mob, but were met with a rain of bottles, stones, lumps of lead, hammerheads and other missiles.

In October and November of that year a national hunger march arrived in London from the north of England. Two thousand five hundred people had walked hundreds of miles, over several weeks, to express their outrage at the lack of work and consequent poverty. A crowd of 100 000 welcomed them in Hyde Park. The *New Statesman* described what happened next 'Suddenly for no apparent reason, the mounted police, accompanied by foot police, began to charge the crowd right and left . . . unemployed and innocent spectators and passers-by.'

More disturbances followed when the marchers attempted to deliver a petition to the Houses of Parliament on 1 November. The focus of the discontent was the National government's decision to impose a means test on the unemployment benefit which necessitated people completing a complex questionnaire about many aspects of their personal life. This procedure saved the government £30 million as many people lost their unemployment benefit.

The MCC Committee made a number of gestures to help the unemployed. Old equipment was donated to charities and net practices were arranged for men on the dole. The latter proved highly successful. William Findlay, the MCC Secretary, wrote to Sir Charles Bright on 8 February 1933, 'The nets for the unemployed seem to be popular. They are a nice lot of fellows and appreciate any little attention.'

The MCC could be as patronising to the twelve professionals they chose to tour Australia and New Zealand as they were to the unemployed, but the players must have been grateful for well-paid work during the English winter. Although the future might not be secure for a professional cricketer, working conditions were preferable to those of

49

the ordinary working-class person whose background he shared. Maurice Leyland, the Yorkshire professional, is quoted in Wilmot's *Defending the Ashes* as commenting:

> I'm a carpenter but I'm a lucky lad. I've had two trips to Australia, I get good wages for playing cricket, and I'll get a benefit in Yorkshire soon, and then I'll buy a business. That's better than being a carpenter. And 'Ducky' and Harold Larwood, and Bill Voce and Tommy Mitchell; they're coal miners. They're better playing cricket.

Mineworkers had suffered a cut in wages after the 1926 general strike and were still much worse off than the great majority of skilled workers, with a weekly wage a little in excess of £2 in 1933. For many, however, the choice was often cricket or the dole. In those economic conditions a professional cricketer could not risk stepping out of line with his County committee or, if a test player, with the MCC Committee. Only an amateur, like Allen, could afford to tell Jardine that he would refuse to bowl bodyline.

In remuneration for undertaking the seven-month Australian tour in 1932–33, the two co-managers were paid £500, the twelve professionals £400 and the five amateurs given an allowance of £150. The MCC met hotel expenses. Upon returning to England the players were given further payments and gifts. The Committee meeting on 29 May 1933 decided that Jardine, Palairet and Warner could purchase souvenirs to the value of £100 and the other amateurs to a maximum of £50 each. An additional £100 was set aside for momentos for all the players and managers.

The professionals received extra bonus payments for discipline and merit. In the same way as amateur captains, like Lord Hawke, would make special one-off payments to particular professional players for specific achievements, so the MCC, on Jardine's recommendations, gave all the professionals £175 each for discipline during the tour. The merit money was allocated as follows: Hammond, Larwood and Sutcliffe—£175 each; Ames, Duckworth, Leyland, Paynter, Verity and Voce—£125 each; Bowes, Mitchell and Tate—£75 each. The Committee had felt inclined to be more generous. They proposed that Ames and Leyland should also receive the full £175 for merit but Jardine would only agree if Hammond, Larwood and Sutcliffe received an extra payment to maintain the differential. The Committee dropped the idea. Out of a total of £4000 which the Committee had made available, £3600 was paid in bonuses to the professionals.

As the main tour party had returned home later than scheduled the MCC felt obliged to make up the professionals' lost match fees. These reimbursements give an illuminating insight into the basic payments a leading international cricket professional might receive in the 1930s. In a week when they played a first class match they could expect between £9 and £11 10s. The amount varied from county to county but the Yorkshire players appear to have been the best paid professionals within the England party. In a week with no first class match, the professional cricketer received only ground staff pay which varied between £3 and £4 per week. This put them on par with a skilled male worker in a large industrial city who would have earned between £3 and £3 10s for a 48-hour working week. An unskilled worker would receive at least £1 less.

The Australian players were not professionals but they were paid for playing in state and international matches. In the 1933–34 season New South Wales state cricketers received an allowance of £1 per day for home games and £1 5s for away games, plus a baggage allowance of £1 while on tour. For a test match appearance they could expect £30 per game, and each player in the 1930 and 1934 test tours received £600 plus expenses.

In the early 1930s, county cricket in England faced severe financial difficulties. The 1933 edition of *Wisden* records that during the previous season gate receipts 'fell once again sadly below the average'. Wet summers in 1930 and 1931 had already weakened all but the most financially secure county clubs. By 1933, Worcestershire found it necessary to make an appeal, through the pages of the *Cricketer*, for donations to ensure their continued participation in the County Championship.

The situation did not improve as the decade progressed. The MCC became so concerned that they established a special County Cricket Commission with a brief to investigate the economic plight of the counties. The report gathered statistical and financial information from the clubs for the period 1934–36. This showed there had been a gradual decline in aggregate gross receipts, due to a combination of poor wealth and a falling off in public interest in the game. Of the seventeen counties only Kent, Middlesex and Yorkshire would have been able to survive any sort of emergency without recourse to fund-raising appeals. The Commission felt that certain unnamed clubs were not in a position to continue playing in the County Championship. Without the income generated by the Australia–England test matches the English county scene would have been vastly different with far fewer clubs participating. The 1933 season was one of the more success-ful, in part due to the fine weather, but also because of the renewed interest in cricket generated by the bodyline tour of Australia.

As well as affecting their domestic economies, and thus their workforces, the Great Depression also strained trade and diplomatic relations between England and Australia. World trade dropped by 25 per cent, which for Britain was a devastating blow. British exports fell by 32 per cent in volume terms and by 50 per cent in value over the period 1929–32. On the world market the prices of raw materials and foodstuffs declined dramatically. Australia, as a major exporter of primary products—wool, wheat and butter, found its export earnings plummeting and its debts mounting. In March 1930 the Australian Labor government asked the British government to allow it to defer an interest payment of £2.77 million which was due on a war loan. The matter was referred to the Bank of England which had become seriously concerned about the state of the Australian economy. They insisted that a Bank of England official be sent to assess the situation and give Australia the necessary advice to enable it to put its financial house in order. The man chosen, Sir Otto Niemeyer, arrived in Australia in July 1930.

On 16 June 1930 Dalton, the British Trade Commissioner in Sydney, had written to Eddison at the Department of Overseas Trade in London:

I think we should be doing something to lead Australia to come to us for help, and having achieved that we should expect 'sanctions' in return. I need not elaborate that idea, but I am afraid that unless something of the kind happens, not only may Australia be in imminent danger for a long time of being unable to meet her overseas commitments but we may lose a very valuable opportunity for bringing her back into the fold not only chastened but more appreciative of the value of the imperial tie.

In August Dalton despatched another report:

> The Westminster Bank alone could make Australia default immediately . . . the country is in an appalling mess, worse, much worse, than a few months ago, but not so bad as it will be . . . the country is now absolutely bankrupt . . . but for the imperial idea there would be no nation, there is no justification for equality and they cannot possibly meet their commitments. So why, I ask you, should we take all this lying down?

In December he cabled 'You cannot possibly over-estimate in your own mind the serious present situation so that you should be prepared to accept anything.' On 24 August the London *Observer* commented: 'There seems to have been a decision by the British money market, to put it bluntly, that Australia must be taught a lesson.'

Dalton's strategy was to exploit the difficult economic circumstances in order to exert pressure on Australia, thereby reinforcing its economic reliance and dependence on Britain. He hoped to impede the desire for greater autonomy which had become more manifest during the 1920s. Australia, Canada and South Africa had pressed at the 1926 Imperial Conference for the status of the Dominions to be redefined as 'autonomous communities within the British Empire, equal in status' although 'united by a common allegiance to the Crown'.

Britain's position as the world's principal trading nation and leading banker had been undermined during, and since, the First World War. This irreversible trend was reflected in the growing share that the United States claimed of the Australian import market. Between 1913 and 1929 the US proportion increased from 14 per cent to 24 per cent, while Britain's declined from 52 per cent to 43 per cent. In July 1925, for the first time, Australia raised a loan of £100 million on the New York money markets when the City of London found themselves unable to meet the Australian requirement.

British manufactured goods were also being challenged on the Australian market by new local products. The boom in Australian manufacturing peaked in the mid-1920s after considerable amounts of local capital had been invested. By 1931–32 the annual value of Australian manufactured goods stood at £281 million which was well in excess of the equivalent sum for local primary produce. To protect its own manufacturers against foreign competition the Labor government, elected in 1928 and led by James Scullin, imposed a series of high protectionist tariffs on imported goods. No exception was made for British items. In April 1930 the Labor government introduced a special customs surcharge of 50 per cent on 132 imports and prohibited 78 other non-essentials. The following year a further 10-per-cent primage duty was levied on all imported goods. The Australian market was heavily protected, to the anger and consternation of traditional British exporters.

One of the items affected was cricket balls. In *Quilt Winders and Pod Shavers* Hugh Barty-King describes the consequences for the British cricket ball manufacturers:

> the cheaper Australian produce almost entirely excluded British cricket balls from the export market. Duke were, in fact, compelled to dismiss a large number of their employees as a result of the Australian Government's tariff imposed on cricket balls in 1930—and so were Wisden in Tonbridge. When in addition Duke cut wages by ten per cent in view of the slackness of trade—exports had been reduced by fifty per cent—the two hundred man work force at Chiddingstone Causeway went on strike.

Sir Otto Niemeyer, the Bank of England emmisary, held the view that Australia was, and should remain, a primary producing country and not endeavour to create a manufacturing sector artificially. He argued that because of import tariffs the producers of primary goods found their costs of production excessively high. He advocated an end to Australian protectionism. Further, he proposed that each state should balance its budget by implementing measures such as a 20-per-cent wage reduction, a cessation of overseas borrowing until all the short-term debts had been cleared and for debt repayments to be paid from revenue and not by further borrowing. The Niemeyer visit ended in November 1930 but the political storm it provoked continued to reverberate around the country after his departure.

Niemeyer's most vocal opponent was the New South Wales Labour Premier J.T. Lang, known to his opponents such as the London *Daily Telegraph* as the 'mad dog', and to his many admirers as the 'big fella' or even Australia's Lenin. Lang argued that Niemeyer was a symbol of 'London financial imperialism' who had been sent to 'foreclose' on Australia. His speeches fuelled the sentiments of Australian nationalism as opposed to the more traditional Anglo-Australian Empire loyalty. At a huge public rally in Sydney on 23 February 1931 he urged: 'Is your vote to go in favour of Sir Otto Niemeyer and his ilk who have said "Let Australia stew in her own juice" . . . Are you Australians? Then strike a blow for yourselves, your homes and your children.'

In 1930 there had been another abrasive exchange between London and Canberra over who was to succeed Lord Stonehaven as Governor-General. The Australian Labor Party felt very strongly that all vice-regal representatives of the British Crown in Australia should be Australian citizens. The Scullin government decided to implement this policy. The traditional procedure, until then, had been for the Dominions Office in London, in collaboration with the King or Queen, to present the Australian government with a short list from which to make a choice. On this occasion Scullin took the intiative and proposed that the position be filled by Sir Isaac Isaacs, the 75-year-old Australian Chief Justice. King George V was horrified. He 'didn't know' Isaacs. As far as he was concerned this was the work of an 'ill-disposed minority' of 'Trade Unions, Communists and Irish'. Scullin refused to give way and raised the matter at the 1930 Imperial Conference where with the support of Canada and South Africa he finally gained victory. Isaacs became the first Australian born Governor-General.

By January 1931 Australian state and federal government loans in London totalled £550 million and were held by 300 000 individuals. The Scullin government, in conjunction with the state premiers, elaborated a plan to balance their respective budgets. The 'premiers plan' advocated wage cuts and tax increases which to a considerable extent mirrored the Niemeyer proposals. Lang opposed the plan. He was committed to a programme of mild social and political reform and part of his alternative strategy was to default on loan repayments as they fell due on the London market. On 1 April 1932 his New South Wales government deliberately failed to pay £729 251 due to bondholders via the Bank of England and the Westminster Bank. This provoked yet another crisis between London and Australia, and within Australia between the federal government and Lang. J.H. Thomas, the Secretary of State for the Dominions in Britain, strenuously urged the federal

Australian government to pay on behalf of the recalcitrant state or they would risk a disastrous slide in confidence by actual or potential investors.

The Scullin government fell in November 1931 to be replaced by the United Australia Party led by Joe Lyons who, like Ramsay MacDonald in Britain, had split from the Labor Party to form a National government with politicians previously to his right. For many middle-class people, Lyons, with his proclaimed firm intention to balance the budget, was the new saviour.

The Lang government defaulted on a loan repayment again in January 1932 and in May his government was autocratically dismissed by the British-appointed state Governor, Air Vice-Marshal Sir Philip Game (setting a precedent repeated in 1975 with the dismissal of the Whitlam federal Labor Government by the British appointed Governor Sir John Kerr). Lang lost the subsequent election. Via Niemeyer, Britain had succeeded in imposing an economic austerity programme, but via Game they had also removed the one state premier who advocated a radically different solution. Among some sections of the Australian population this sequence of events further impassioned feelings against Britain and the Empire.

The large Australian loans outstanding on the London market required high interest repayments which consumed a considerable and growing portion of the nation's export earnings. After the base rate of interest in London had dropped to 2.5 per cent in June 1932 the Australian government began pressing to be allowed to convert their loans to a new and lower rate of interest. Though the British government began converting its own loans to 3 per cent, and occasionally less, Australia continued to be charged 6 per cent and often slightly more. The discrepancy seemed iniquitous but the British Treasury were adamant that the market could not absorb a major Commonwealth conversion. The conversion loan crisis lurched on until July 1933 when Britain finally acceded to the Australian request, though not before it had influenced the outcome of the bodyline controversy and further strained imperial loyalties.

The Imperial Economic Conference convened in Ottawa from 21 July to 20 August 1932 made an attempt to resolve the growing contradictions within the Empire. The high-powered British delegation included Baldwin, Chamberlain, Thomas and Hailsham. Australia's main representative was Stanley Melbourne Bruce, the former Prime Minister, who was shortly to become resident Minister in London. Protectionism and tariffs emerged as the most important items on the agenda. The British government was prepared to give preference to Dominion imports within the British tariff structure provided the Dominions, in return, made concessions to facilitate greater access for British manufactured goods in their respective home markets. The British had to tread cautiously for fear of upsetting either their own farming communities or their non-Commonwealth trading partners, and while the Dominions wanted to increase the exports of their primary products they also had to protect their own manufacturing sectors from being crushed by competitively priced British imports. Nobody could be completely satisfied.

The final compromise reached gave Dominion foodstuffs an imperial preference on the British market in exchange for British exports receiving favourable treatment in the Dominions. The latter was achieved by the tariffs on all non-British imports being increased. Both Britain and Australia had highly protected economies and the imperial trade war led to many bitter exchanges in the press and letters of complaint to the Dominions Office from disgruntled British manufacturers who claimed they had been unfairly treated in Australia. This did nothing to improve Anglo-Australian relations, already strained by the Niemeyer visit, the Isaacs appointment, the Lang dismissal and the loans crisis.

Many politicians and diplomats hoped that the 1932–33 MCC tour to Australia would help re-establish some harmony and mutual understanding. Others saw the test series as an opportunity to find a new national pride amidst world chaos. For some in Australia cricket was an important aspect in the formation of the emergent nation's identity and self-consciousness. Matches against the 'mother-country' were a yardstick in measuring that growth. For others in London, the tour offered Britain an opportunity to bring the troublesome Dominion 'back into the fold not only chastened but more appreciative' of the imperial tie.

Douglas Jardine recognised the connection between the Ottawa conference and the tour. When the *Orontes* docked in Colombo, en route to

Australia, he took the opportunity to despatch a written forerunner. His message read: 'While our statesmen have drawn closer than ever before, at Ottawa, may the friendly rivalry on the cricket field, our joint national pastime, add its quota of cement to the foundation laid in the past and at Ottawa.' The reality was to be very different.

4
The English response

On 18 January 1933, while the bodyline battle was at its height on the cricket pitch, a small group of Australian Cricket Board delegates present in Adelaide, acting on behalf of the Board, sent this telegram to the MCC Committee in London:

> Bodyline bowling assumed such proportions as to menace best interests of game making protection of body by batsmen the main consideration and causing intensely bitter feelings between players as well as injury. In our opinion it is unsportsmanlike and unless stopped at once is likely to upset the friendly relations existing between Australia and England.

The wording was not universally acclaimed in Australia, let alone England where it was coldly received. 'These gentlemen on the Australian Board of Control are rather tiresome', wrote William Findlay, the full-time MCC Secretary, on 21 January 1933. In another letter the same day he commented, 'It is unfortunate this fuss in Australia. They are very difficult people.'

Before Jardine's team had left England there had already been a number of acrimonious exchanges between Lord's and the Board in Adelaide. In 'the general interest of cricket' the MCC wanted to include a short visit to New Zealand as part of their return journey from Australia. The Board cabled their objection: 'unanimously strongly opposed any inroads Australian tour purpose visiting another country and cannot agree your request regarding New Zealand'. The MCC minutes further record the Committee's opinion that the financial conditions 'did not appear to be in accordance with those of the 1928–29 tour'. Given that several English county clubs were struggling to survive, the revenue generated from the Australian tour was of the utmost importance. Dr Robert MacDonald, the Australian Board's representative in England, was called to headquarters to discuss these two matters with Lord Hawke. The MCC view prevailed.

The Board's telegram was thus not likely to be well-received. Matters were made worse by the fact that the cable appeared in the stop press columns of the English morning papers before it had been officially received at Lord's (the Reuter's cable, sent by Gilbert Mant at priority press rate, preceded the Board's official telegram sent at the ordinary rate). Viscount Lewisham, the MCC President, was roused from his bed at 2.30 a.m. by newspaper reporters asking for his comments on a document he had not seen. The telegram reached London as England were poised to win the third test and the British press were not slow to accuse the Australians of 'squealing', while the charge of 'unsportsmanlike' behaviour made against Jardine's team was certain to upset the predominantly conservative members of the MCC Committee. The Earl of Dartmouth, an elder statesman within the MCC and known as the 'Governor', put his feelings into verse

> We have fought
> We have won
> And we have lost
> But we have never squealed before.

A special meeting of the full MCC Committee was convened on 23 January to agree a reply to the Board. To assist in their deliberations they had before them letters and cables from Jardine, Palairet and Warner. After two hours they concluded and despatched the following cable:

We the Marylebone Cricket Club deplore your cable message and deprecate the opinion that there has been unsportsmanlike play. We have the fullest confidence in our captain team and managers and are convinced that they would do nothing to infringe the laws of cricket or the spirit of the game. We have no evidence that our confidence is misplaced. Much as we regret the accidents to Woodfull and Oldfield we understand that in neither case was the bowler to blame. If the Board wishes to propose a new law or rule it shall receive our careful consideration in due course. We hope that the situation is not now as serious as your cable appears to indicate but if it is such as to jeopardise the good relations between

England and Australian cricketers and you consider it desirable to cancel the remainder of the programme we would consent with great reluctance.

The text of the MCC reply had been written by the President, Viscount Lewisham, and Sir Kynaston Studd, but this final version was the third draft and at each stage the tone had become tougher. Findlay had roughed out the first on 18 January and sent his proposed wording to Lacey:

Much regret contents of your cable. Marylebone assured that no English bowler bowls at the man but at leg stump which is said to be the weakness of certain batsmen. Cricketers of today have not had great experience of fast bowling and the open stance of batsman necessarily increases risk. Of all considerations friendly relations and the game itself paramount. If remaining tests cannot be played in this spirit and appreciated by players and spectators alike would it not be well to consider substitution of state games.

On 20 January Lewisham and Findlay wrote a second draft which appeared basically as before but incorporated a revised final sentence which read: 'If Australian Board consider that Larwood is too fast a bowler to be safe on present Australian wickets Marylebone feel sure that Jardine would give the utmost consideration to their view.' In both these drafts the responsibility for the difficulties was assumed to lie either with the Australian batsmen's technique or the state of the wickets. It is obvious that the Australian Board, or their players, would never accept the indignity of asking Jardine not to play Larwood. They would either be humiliated or their bluff would be called and they would be shown to be 'squealers'.

The significance of the first two drafts is that neither proposed cancelling the remainder of the tour. The source for this idea was a mysterious Lord F. who suggested to Findlay that we 'give them a rap across the knuckles' and cancel the last two tests. Findlay recounts this in a rather light-hearted manner in a letter to Sir Kynaston Studd on 20 January. Studd must have taken the idea more seriously as it appeared in the final text which he had co-written. When the Committee met on 23 January the *Daily Mail* described the atmosphere at Lord's 'as near an approach to that of Downing Street on the eve of a great national crisis as one could imagine'. The future of Anglo-Australian test cricket now hung in the balance.

Who were the members of the MCC Committee, controlling the destiny of imperial cricket from St John's Wood in London? Although the Committee included eighteen members, the crucial proposals and decisions on bodyline were made by an inner group of six, plus Findlay, who as Secretary did not have a vote on the Committee. The sextet were the President Viscount Lewisham, the Treasurer Lord Hawke, Viscount Bridgeman, Sir Francis Lacey, Sir Stanley Jackson and Sir Kynaston Studd.

Viscount Lewisham, born the Hon. William Legge and subsequently the seventh Earl of Dartmouth, had a long aristocratic lineage. In 1933 he was 51 which made him considerably younger than the other five. He had been a Conservative MP for eight years (1910–18) and from 1928 onwards held the office of Lord Great Chamberlain of England. His father, Lord Dartmouth, and his grandfather were both past presidents of the MCC.

Lord Hawke, born the Hon. Martin Bladen, was the seventh Baron Hawke. Although a fervent Yorkshireman all his life he was born in Lincolnshire and became one of the rare breed of Yorkshire players whose birthplace was outside the county. In his autobiography, *Recollections and Reminiscences*, Hawke bemoans the lack of a family fortune, though he and his brothers, with one exception, all went to Eton. Ten years before his death Martin's country gentleman father became a 'city man', joining the Boards of Directors of the Buenos' Ayres Southern Railway, the Direct United States Cable Company and the Taltal Railway. This was a typical development in the latter half of the nineteenth century as the landed aristocracy were slowly integrated into the citadels of manufacturing capital and the shrines to foreign investment. According to Martin his father was 'a perfect Sahib'.

The seventh Baron Hawke took his seat in the House of Lords in 1888 but by 1924 had still not made his maiden speech. Apart from cricket his other interests included golf, hunting big game, billiards—which he played left-handed whereas he batted right-handed—letter writing and music. As a director of the Academy of Music he prefered the waltz to what he chose to call 'nigger dances'. He held strong views on most subjects and cricket, the game he loved above all others, was no exception. In his autobiography he explained what he saw as the prime

Lord Hawke in his younger days

attributes of both hunting and cricket: 'High and low, rich and poor, greet one another practically on an equality, and sad will be the day for England if socialism ever succeeds in putting class v. class and thus ending sports which have made England.'

Hawke's reign as Yorkshire captain lasted from 1883 until 1910. He assumed the Presidency of the County Club in 1898 which he retained until his death in 1938. As a player he was not a great batsman. Only on one occasion did he score 1000 runs in a season and his career batting average is fractionally below 20. Little is remembered of his bowling and the records show that he took just one first-class wicket. However, under his firm and autocratic leadership Yorkshire won the County Championship eight times. His team was sustained by professionals of the highest calibre, such as David Denton, Schofield Haigh, George Hirst and Wilfred Rhodes, to name only four. As a disciplinarian Hawke had no equals. Both Edmund Peate and Bobby Peel, successive slow left-arm bowlers for the county, were dismissed from the professional staff as a consequence of their partiality to beer.

Hawke was President of the MCC for the duration of the First World War and after the death of Lord Harris in 1932 he took on the responsibilities of Treasurer. He then became the dominant and most influential figure at Lord's and within the MCC Committee. Pelham Warner in *Lord's*, describes Hawke as follows:

For one who had travelled so far and done so much for Dominion and Colonial cricket, it was curious that he was not always anxious to welcome Australian teams. He was fearful of the demands on his Yorkshiremen: he loved Yorkshire too well. It may be that on occasions he made speeches that were carelessly phrased and which did not convey his exact meaning.

Viscount Bridgeman, born William Clive Bridgeman, became a Conservative MP in 1906 and represented Oswestry until 1929. He attained high office. Having been made a Privy Councillor in 1920 he became Home Secretary in 1922. Serving under Stanley Baldwin, the cricket-loving Prime Minister, he was given the position of First Lord of the Admiralty in 1924 and he retained the portfolio for the subsequent five years. He was President of the MCC in 1931.

Sir Francis Lacey, known as 'Ben', was knighted in 1926 after serving as the MCC Secretary for 28 years. He had qualified as a barrister, but apart from playing cricket for Hampshire as an amateur, worked for the MCC. Warner describes his manner as being 'at times a little cold and official, and perhaps over-rigid in interpretation of rules and regulations'. In 1932–33 Lacey was not a member of the Committee but remained central to all decisions taken due to his position as Trustee.

Sir Stanley Jackson, the son of Lord Allerton, became one of the great cricketer-politicians. 'Jacker', as he was often called, went to Harrow where he had Baldwin as a friend and contemporary and Winston Churchill as his fag. Jackson quickly emerged as one of the great amateur batsman of the 'Golden Age' of cricket in pre-war England. Playing for Yorkshire, he scored more than 10 000 runs in dashing style and claimed over 500 wickets. With the omnipresent Hawke leading Yorkshire he had little opportunity to captain his county although he was given that responsibility for England against Australia in 1905. Service in the Boer War interrupted his cricket for two years at the turn of the century.

As a Conservative MP for Howdenshire in Yorkshire (1915–26) he worked for a short period in the War Office, but in 1923 became Chairman of the Conservative Party. In 1926 he was nominated to the Privy Council and the following year chosen to be the Governor of Bengal. The five years, (1927–32) he spent in India were marked by considerable political unrest as the nationalist movement continued to grow and expand its influence under the leadership of Gandhi's Congress Party.

In Bengal, Jackson had to contend with a Congress Party, led by Subhas Chandra Bose, which was more radical and aggressive. The year after Jackson arrived there was a general strike in the Calcutta jute mills involving hundreds of thousands of workers. The political ferment and social unrest continued throughout his period in Bengal. In 1930 and 1931 a number of leading public figures were assassinated including the Inspector General of Police, the Superintendent of Police, a district Magistrate and a sessions Judge. Shortly before his departure for England in 1932 an attempt was made on Jackson's life when five shots were fired at him from close range but all missed.

Within the MCC Committee there seems to have been concern over Jackson's lack of discretion. Of all the members he was the most often quoted in the press. In a letter of 27 January 1933 Findlay comments

Sir Stanley Jackson

66

that he was 'fearful' about remarks that Jackson might make in public about the bodyline crisis. Warner expresses similar doubts in a letter to Findlay in November 1934:—'I am at a loss re-Jacker. What a wobbler he is . . . What is wrong with Jacker? He supports a recommendation in committee and then has doubts later. His mentality beats me.'

Sir Kynaston Studd was one of six sons of a father who was an indigo planter in Bihar and a mother from a Calcutta merchant family. The Studds became reknowned as a cricketing family after Kynaston and two of his brothers played in the same Cambridge University eleven in 1881 and 1882. Studd abandoned the idea of going into the family firm in the City of London in order to train as a medical missionary but nothing came of this. In 1885 Quintin Hogg, the father of the first Lord Hailsham, asked Studd to work with him in establishing the Regent Street Polytechnic in London. Studd became Honorary Secretary, later Vice-President, and then President in 1903 when Hogg died—a post he occupied until his death in 1944. From 1923 onwards he was an Alderman for the City of London and in 1928–29 its Lord Mayor.

Of the inner group of six all, except Jackson and Lacey, were educated at Eton. Jackson was a Harrow boy and Lacey went to a slightly less prestigious public school, Sherborne. Bridgeman, Hawke, Jackson, Lacey and Studd all went to Cambridge University, Lewisham's university career was spent at Oxford. Two were Privy Councillors. Three had been Members of Parliament.

Friendship had bonded this sextet together over the years. Hawke, Studd and Lacey played cricket together for Cambridge University in the early 1880s. Bridgeman gained his cricket blue at Cambridge in 1887. Jackson began representing Yorkshire, under the captaincy of Hawke, as early as 1890, while he was still studying at Cambridge and leading the University eleven. Bridgeman, Hawke and Jackson were members of the Conservative Carlton Club, which included amongst its members several other MCC Committee members as well as half of all the Conservative MPs sitting in the House of Commons. The Carlton Club was exclusive and expensive: the membership fee was £40 and the annual subscription 17 guineas. More significantly it was at such clubs that the ruling class discussed and elaborated a view on world and national politics. The MCC Committee usually met at the Junior Carlton Club.

The sextet was not the only notable figures on the MCC Committee in 1933. Among the other members were Lord Aberdare, who combined membership of the Conservative Party, the right wing Anglo-German Fellowship and the International Olympic Committee; Lord Hampden, who was head of one of the country's great landed aristocratic families, Lord-Lieutenant of Hertfordshire and Lord in Waiting to King George V; the Earl of Lucan, another former Conservative MP who for most of the 1920s was aide-de-camp to the King; and Viscount Ullswater, barrister, Privy Councillor, and former Tory MP who for sixteen years, until 1921, served as Speaker in the House of Commons.

The Committee was leavened by a number of men with cricketing, rather than political or aristocratic, backgrounds: for example Percy Chapman, the England captain during the 1928 MCC tour to Australia; 'Shrimp' Leveson-Gower, the Surrey President; Lt-Colonel Heseltine, the Hampshire President; Dick Palairet, the former Surrey Secretary; and Pelham Warner. After 'careful consideration', to quote Lord Hawke, the latter two had been appointed joint managers of the 1932–33 tour.

Findlay, the Secretary, had been a cricket administrator for 26 years. He had been educated at Eton and Oriel College, Oxford, and had captained both his school and university cricket teams. After going down from Oxford in 1903 he played cricket as wicket-keeper for Lancashire before becoming the Secretary of Surrey. Shortly after the end of the First World War he moved to Lord's to undertake the responsibilities of Assistant to the then Secretary, Francis 'Ben' Lacey, succeeding to the secretaryship when Lacey retired in 1926. In that position he earned a reputation for charm, courtesy and industry.

This, then, was the MCC Committee in 1933—drawn from the best families, educated at the finest public schools and universities, closely involved with the Conservative Party and strongly loyal to the Empire. The Committee was a mirror image of the landed British ruling class, and to be a club member was to display the social and cultural credentials of that class.

It is very noticeable that the leading members of the MCC Committee were drawn from the aristocracy and not the industrial and manufacturing sections of the ruling class. There is a striking similarity in the personal histories and backgrounds of Lewisham, Hawke, Jackson, Bridgeman, Hampden, Lucan and Ullswater. These were men whose wealth came from the land, who identified with the Empire, and whose values were inherently Victorian and conservative.

The English response

Thomas Hughes in *Tom Brown's Schooldays*, that classic account of public school life written in 1857, expressed the Victorian's view of cricket: 'But it's more than a game. It's an institution' said Tom. 'Yes,' said Arthur, 'the birthright of British boys old and young as habeas corpus and trial by jury are of British men.'

Through the Empire the British forcibly exported their goods, their laws and their sports. Of the last-named cricket was the most important. By 1890 cricket and the Empire had become synonymous. Lord Harris put it succinctly when he said 'Cricket had done more to consolidate the Empire than any other influence.'

The game became an integral part of the Anglicisation of the colonies, to such an extent that Neville Cardus could later write, 'Where the English language is unspoken there can be no real cricket.'

The period of the 'Golden Age' of English cricket, from 1890 until 1914, coincided with the final decades of undisputed British trade and military dominance in the world. It was also during those years that the 1933 MCC Committee had their hey-day as youngish men on the sports fields and parade grounds. In the pre-war years the rich had filled their leisure hours with country house parties, yachting, shooting, luxury travel and cricket. The amateur player, usually as a batsman, reigned supreme. During the 1905 English county season amateur batsmen scored 49 per cent of all runs but bowled only 20 per cent of the total number of overs delivered. For many amateurs, bowling was 'donkey work' to be undertaken by the professionals, although Lord Harris who held the professional cricketer in high regard often polemicised against this view.

Amateur status, being 'a gentleman', 'not trying too hard', 'playing the game', accepting defeat graciously, never questioning an umpire's decision, expressing modesty in victory: these were all established as the basic tenets of sportsmanlike behaviour. To act otherwise was not cricket. These values became a central component of the education of the rich in the public schools. The games-dominated curriculum, allied to an overt anti-intellectualism, contributed to a decline in the British economy that was evident even prior to 1914. This was the consequence of an education policy dating back 60 years, during which Gladstone had declared:

The relation of pure science, natural science, modern languages, modern history and the rest to the old classical training, ought to be founded on a principle ... I deny their right to a parallel or equal position; their true position is ancillary, and as ancillary it ought to be limited and restrained without scruples.

In 1872 there were only twelve students taking natural science examinations at Cambridge University. In 1913 Britain had only 9000 university students, whereas there were almost 60 000 in Germany. In comparison to the other industrial nations the British secondary and tertiary education system lagged far behind, failing to meet the needs of manufacturing industry. Education in Britain reflected the values of the landed aristocracy, society had become conservative and complacent, and in this cricket played an integral part.

Family circumstances allowed men like Hawke and Warner the opportunity to devote their lives to cricket. Pelham Warner, having gained his cricket blue in 1895 and a third-class honours degree in jurisprudence the following year, left Oxford University to become permanently engaged in playing, writing or administrating cricket. He was the ideologue of the 'Golden Age' with a set of high morals.

Towards the end of the 1932 county season, Warner was upset by a particular incident. Bill Bowes, playing for Yorkshire against Surrey, had bowled short on the leg-side with a packed on-side field. Writing in the *Morning Post* for whom he was cricket correspondent, Warner spoke out forthrightly:

Bowes must alter his tactics. Bowes bowled with five men on the on-side and sent down several very short pitched balls which repeatedly bounced head high and more. Now that it is not bowling; indeed it is not cricket; and if all the fast bowlers were to adopt his methods, MCC would be compelled to step in and penalise the bowler.

Bowes's tactics in this match were, in essence, the same as bodyline bowling, and thus Warner's condemnation of this type of bowling was publicly on record prior to the MCC team's departure. Despite Warner's strictures Bowes was added to the MCC party at the last moment. The tour selection sub-committee of Hawke, Warner, Perrin, Higson and Jardine as captain had been meeting during the summer. They had picked the two sides for the Gentlemen v. Players game at

Lord's in July 1932 and included twelve of the seventeen in the subsequent tour party. Bowes was not among them. His name was included after the controversial Yorkshire v. Surrey match in which Jardine had captained Surrey. Hawke was President of Bowes' county club, Yorkshire. Not everybody at Lord's favoured the inclusion of Bowes. On 5 January 1933 Findlay expressed the opinion, in a letter, that Bowes was 'not good enough' to have made the tour.

On several occasions during the Australian tour Warner, in his capacity as co-manager and MCC emissary, made speeches about the sporting attributes of cricket. Shortly after arriving in Australia he said:

> The very word cricket has become a synonym for all that is true
> and honest. To say 'that is not cricket' implies something
> underhand, something not in keeping with the best ideals. There is
> no game which calls forth so many fine attributes, which makes so
> many demands on its votaries, and, that being so, all who love it as
> players, or officials, or spectators, must be careful lest anything
> they do should do it harm . . . This is the aim of the Marylebone
> Cricket Club—of which I am a humble if devoted servant—in
> sending teams to all parts of the world to spread the gospel of
> British fair play as developed in its national sport.

Warner was a leading member of the MCC Committee and a member of the on-tour selection committee, along with Jardine and Sutcliffe. Prior to the party's departure the MCC Committee had decided that the on-tour selection committee would be Warner, Jardine and Sutcliffe, and also that no player would be nominated as vice-captain, although Wyatt did assume the captaincy in Jardine's absence. During the tour, at Jardine's instigation, Wyatt and Hammond were added to the selection committee. Given that Warner and Wyatt have always claimed that they opposed bodyline and that Sutcliffe was known to be a strong supporter of Jardine, it can be assumed that at least during the tour Hammond advocated bodyline or did not raise any objection to it.

Throughout the tour the Warner spirit was overwhelmed by Jardine's 'win at all costs' approach. Jardine was too strong a character for the physically frail Warner who claims to have pleaded for moderation on several occasions. But by allowing Jardine complete control over the cricket tactics Warner abrogated his responsibilities as tour manager and above all, to the game itself. In retrospect, his only other course of action would have been to offer his resignation and appeal to the authority of the MCC Committee. 'Plum apparently has not told Jardine that he does not approve of this kind of bowling', Findlay told Lacey in a letter on 18 January 1933. The source for this information is unclear but must have been either Palairet or Jardine himself both of whom were writing regularly to Findlay. More importantly for the future of the tour it highlights the fact that Warner lacked the courage of his convictions or else was keeping all his options open. Instead, he gained the reputation for being a weak man who wanted to be liked by everybody.

When the Australian Board made the justifiable claim that bodyline represented 'unsportsmanlike' behaviour they attacked, almost certainly unwittingly, the very essence of the British way of life. To make such an accusation about an MCC team, which as Warner said 'spread the gospel of British fair play', challenged cricket, the Empire, the MCC and its Committee's values. The members of the MCC Committee could not conceive that an amateur captain was not 'playing the game'.

Jardine had voiced his concern that headquarters would not support him if, and when, the going got tough. His concern was misplaced, although it has to be said that the deliberations of the Committee were, in part, determined by the reports that Jardine himself was despatching from Australia. When the MCC Committee met on 23 January they had before them letters and cables from Jardine, Palairet and Warner. Dick Palairet's views on bodyline have never been publicly known but it is now generally assumed that he supported Jardine who was captain at Surrey while Palairet was secretary. This would explain why Palairet felt it necessary to submit a separate report to that of Warner's, which was critical of Jardine's bodyline tactics.

These reports are not available in the Lord's archives, but small fragments are quoted in Findlay's correspondence. In a letter to Lacey he quotes from Jardine:

So far our bowling has in general been a shock and an unpleasant surprise to the old hands of Australia. The papers have put up a squeal rising to a whine about bowling at the man. Nothing of the sort, but we have by dint of hard work and, I hope, clear thinking got a field suitable for attacking the leg stump.

Jardine had written these remarks on 13 December 1932 shortly after the first test in Sydney, the seventh first-class game on the tour. The tone and style do not indicate a sudden discovery of an Australian batting weakness and new England bowling tactics, on the contrary it reads rather that Jardine's well-prepared strategy and thinking had come to fruition.

On 12 December Warner sent Findlay a letter which expressed a view contrary to Jardine's. He stated that 'It would be silly to disregard the hostile feeling which has been created by this type of bowling . . . one of these days there will be a terrible accident.'

Findlay, although not a voting member of the Committee, was a person with considerable influence at Lord's. From his correspondence it is clear he was confused by the conflicting evidence coming from Australia. On 18 January he wrote in one letter: 'Jardine seems to have captained the side splendidly', while in another: 'This leg bowling, as practised by Bowes is not what we want to see.' Two days later, on 20 January, Findlay commented in a letter to Viscount Ullswater: 'Personally I hope and believe they will support Jardine', while the same day he could also write to Lord Bridgeman: 'Personally I hate these five men on the leg-side but I cannot believe that the Australian Board and the spectators are not squealing.'

The MCC Committee and Findlay were not being given a true picture of events by Jardine but nor do they seem to have made any effort to substantiate the press reports of bodyline bowling after the third test in Adelaide. The British press did carry some views which were strongly critical of bodyline and the MCC could have used the recently established telephonic communication link with Australia to seek clarification. There are no indications that they took that option— after all, they were two-to-one up in the fight to win the Ashes.

Sir Stanley Jackson made a number of confused and contradictory remarks in public. Presumably unaware of the extent to which Jardine was employing bodyline and the packed, close leg-side field, Jacker made two implicit, criticisms of the England tactics, which were quoted in the press. On 19 January the London *Daily Telegraph* reported him as saying:

> If leg theory bowling had been used to any degree cricket could
> not have lasted in its present form. I firmly believe that if it

became common for fast bowlers to use this method of attack it would ruin the game. Cricket does not depend for its prosperity and popularity on written, but on unwritten laws.

Jackson's words were prophetic. Bodyline, pioneered in the test arena, had already begun to spread into the Australian parks. The weekend after the Adelaide test the Melbourne *Herald* claimed that bodyline was commonplace. On one Saturday afternoon four people were hurt in local matches and a fight had broken out between a bowler and a batsman. Local schools took swift action and banned bodyline bowling. On 2 February the *West Australian* carried a report that Merv Inverarity, the father of Australian test player John Inverarity, had made an official complaint to the West Australian Cricket Association about the bodyline tactics of Ron Halcombe in a local grade match. Halcombe had previously been at the centre of a throwing controversy when serious doubts had been raised over his action.

As Jackson had pointed out, bodyline was not formally against any of the laws of cricket. Jardine contravened an unwritten code of morals and ethics whose origins lay in the public schools and English cricket's so called 'Golden Age' prior to the 1914 War. Jardine's ruthless desire to win at all costs may have clashed with the Warner spirit but it did not break any rules. On 26 January Jackson was quoted in the *Guardian*: 'My advice is play the game as we knew it in the past and the trouble will end.' His own confusion is obvious for in the same breath he urged 'backing our people in Australia'. It would be several months before he found himself able to resolve these dilemmas.

Lord Hawke began by wondering 'What would George have done?' — George being Lord Harris, the other great autocratic figure at Lord's, who had died the previous year. In public, Lord Hawke made almost no comment on the Adelaide incidents in particular or bodyline in general, but on 19 January he is quoted in the *Guardian* as remonstrating, 'Remember the 1921 tests'. That series in England had also been marked by acrimony. The Australian fast bowling combination of Gregory and McDonald had bruised the ribs of several English players and there were at least two off-the-field incidents which continued to rankle with the English cricketing establishment.

The MCC had sent a team to Australia in 1920–21 and England had lost all five tests in an unprecedented series of defeats. The Australians visited England in 1921 and proceeded to win the first three tests to make it eight wins in succession. The fourth and the fifth tests were drawn, the former due to rain and the latter in farcical circumstances as England batted out time. Warwick Armstrong, the huge Australian captain, had an arrogant victorious air and on two occasions he clashed with the MCC. The first occured at Manchester in the fourth test and was described in the 1922 edition of *Wisden* as 'humiliating' for England and their captain the Hon. Lionel Tennyson. Tennyson and his advisors in the pavilion blundered over a point of law and illegally tried to declare the England innings. Armstrong promptly pointed out the error and insisted that England continue to bat.

The second took place when the Australians met an MCC eleven at Lord's. The hours of play were to have been 12.00 to 6.00. The MCC announced them in the press as being until 6.30 and compounded the mistake by printing it on the scorecard. Armstrong refused to accept any changes and the MCC were forced to concede. A Committee meeting was called and a public apology issued but, as Warner wrote in his book, *Lord's*, published in 1946:

It was not wise or tactful to force the MCC to issue an apology to the public, and the general opinion was that the MCC should have insisted on normal hours of play at Lord's being kept . . . The headquarters of cricket should not have been treated in so cavalier a manner.

It is worth remembering that at the time Hawke was a leading figure on the Committee, Lacey was the MCC Secretary and Jackson the outgoing President.

In January 1933 after the Australian Board had accused England of being 'unsportsmanlike' the MCC Committee closed ranks behind Jardine. Sir Stanley Jackson, speaking at the Yorkshire Annual General Meeting on 25 January, expressed the Committee's sentiments: 'It was absolutely essential that we should back up our own people, for it was impossible for us to think that the men we know could have resorted to any method of cricket injurious to the general interests of the game.' Lord Hampden, another Committee member, reinforced the point when he said: 'There is no reason why we should not trust those on the spot and we can only suppose that the Australian contentions are exaggerated.' The MCC now awaited the outcome of the Australian Board's meeting on Monday 30 January 1933 in Sydney. Because of the distances between the state capitals in Australia, the travelling time and the cost of Board meetings were great. This seven-hour meeting was the only occasion during the bodyline crisis that the Board members were able to meet together to discuss the issues and formulate a policy.

Prior to the Board meeting in Australia two significant events occured in London. First the MCC received a letter of support from Stanley Baldwin, the leader of the Conservative Party, in which he expressed his pleasure at the Committee's cable. At first glance this endorsement from Baldwin may not seem particularly important but it should be remembered that he was the de facto leader of the National government. Although the Prime Minister was the former Labour leader, Ramsay MacDonald, the National government relied for its support on the Tory Party: 471 of the 615 MPs were Conservatives and Baldwin, as Party leader, was the dominant figure in British politics. Baldwin had been at school and university with several of the Committee members or knew them via Conservative Party circles. Unsurprisingly too, he was a member of the Carlton Club.

The second event occured on 26 January 1933 when an official telegram arrived at the Dominions Office for Sir Alexander Hore-Ruthven, the Governor of South Australia who was on leave in England. The cable, from South Australia, read: 'A hint from Marylebone to Jardine to publicly state that fast bowling leg field will be abandoned rest of tour will probably restore good feeling all around.' It forms the first entry in the file on bodyline which the Dominions Office opened. The index to this file still exists at the Public Records Office in London although it is held in a register closed to the public. The file, reference number F 20436/2, lists 43 entries until June 1934 but unfortunately the contents of the file have not been preserved.

Given the public position of the Committee and the private views of its leading members it would have been impossible for the MCC to accept the terms being suggested from South Australia. To have done so would have been a clear rebuke for Jardine. On 27 January the Dominions Office sent copies of the Hore-Ruthven cable to Viscounts Lewisham and Ullswater, Lord Bridgeman and Sir Kynaston Studd. An official communication between the Governor of South Australia and his deputy in Adelaide was thus circulated by the Dominions Office to non-official personnel. Although formally incorrect, this was the reality of many government decisions.

The following day Bridgeman, Ullswater and Lewisham all sent replies. Further telegrams were despatched to Lord Hawke and Viscount Lewisham on 30 January and to Hore-Ruthven and Sir Stanley Jackson on 31 January. Hawke and Jackson replied on 31 January and finally, on 1 February, a reply went off to South Australia. The contents of this flurry of telegrams remain a mystery but it proves that the Dominions Office was seriously involved in the controversy from an early stage and considerably before it was prepared to admit its complicity publicly.

After a quiet weekend the scene was set for a series of dramatic meetings, feverish phone calls and further telegrams. The fourth test was due to begin on Friday, 10 February in Brisbane. Would it take place? How quickly could the damage to Anglo-Australian cricket and diplomatic relations be repaired? There were eleven days before the first ball was due to be bowled.

Sir Alexander Gore Arkwright Hore-Ruthven, Sandy to his friends, was another Eton boy. From Britain's premier public school he went directly into the Highland Light Infantry. For 30 years he led a military life—a Victoria Cross won in the Sudan, two trips to Australia with Lords Dudley and Kitchener, severly wounded at Gallipoli, Commander of the Welsh Guards and finally the 1st Infantry Brigade. Lifelong member of the MCC. In 1928 he was appointed Governor of South Australia.

Fully aware of the more general political consequences of the bodyline crisis, he went to see J.H. Thomas, the Secretary of State for the Dominions on Tuesday, 31 January. Later that day he had lunch with William Findlay. Thomas had left the Labour Party with Ramsay MacDonald to help form the National government. He had little interest in cricket, his sporting associations being with the turf. As a consequence of this informal conversation, he decided to convene a small conference of interested parties. He invited Hore-Ruthven, Sir Thomas Inskip, who was a keen cricketer, a member of the MCC and the Attorney-General in the government, and four representatives of the MCC Committee. The meeting took place in Downing Street on 1 February.

The MCC quartet Viscount Lewisham, Sir Kynaston Studd,

Sir Alexander Hore-Ruthven (later Lord Gowrie)

Viscount Bridgeman and Sir Stanley Jackson, reported on the latest developments. Lord's had received four new cables from the Australian Board, Jardine, Palairet and Warner, which kept them abreast of the most recent events in Australia. The Australian Board had sent a telegram which rejected any idea of cancelling the remainder of the tour, but failed to withdraw the offending word, 'unsportsmanlike'. Jardine informed them of a unanimous decision taken at a meeting of the players. Findlay in a letter to Viscount Ullswater, dated 3 February, explains: 'we had received a cable from the team wishing to cancel the remainder of the tour unless the Australian Board withdrew the word "unsportsmanlike"'. This was considerably more serious than the Australian and British press speculation that Jardine was threatening to refuse to captain the England team or that the amateurs would not play in the fourth test by way of a protest. For all seventeen players to demand the cancellation of the tour and their immediate return to England would have been a significant blow to the already poor Anglo-Australian sporting and diplomatic relations. Warner told of his attempts to solve the crisis. After very considerable pressure from the team he and Palairet had requested the assistance of Ernest Crutchley, the British government's representative in Canberra. Warner was also engaged in discussions with J.S. Hutcheon and R.J. Hartigan, the two Queensland representatives on the Australian Board who had both opposed the despatching of the Board's first telegram.

The Dominions Office gave no official explanation for the Downing Street meeting with the MCC. When questioned about it, Thomas grinned broadly, and added: 'It is leg pulling rather than leg bowling'. He was very keen to deny any liason with Ernest Crutchley. Hore-Ruthven commented that his part was 'purely personal and informal' and that he prefered 'to say nothing about it'. Thomas and the Dominions Office did later admit that they had allowed the MCC to use the diplomatic cipher codes to communicate with Warner and Jardine in Australia. On 2 February Crutchley wrote to Warner and expressed his dismay at the 'damnable' leakage, within the Post Office, of a cable Warner had sent from Sydney. Crutchley commented: 'I feared the worst directly I saw your telegram in clear'.

Six months later Thomas did mention the political significance of the bodyline crisis—at a luncheon in Claridges on 11 August for Sir Julian Cahn's cricket touring party which was about to sail for Canada. The setting was bizarre. In the middle of the dining room a 22-yard strip had been laid out in the form of a wicket and around the room the tables were arranged in fielding positions. The *Daily Telegraph* carried a picture of those seated at the short-leg table. The waiters wore flannels which complemented the green decor. Thomas made a short farewell speech after drinking too much champagne.

> My job as Dominions Secretary is to reconcile the different
> elements in the British Commonwealth. When you remember that
> that includes South Africa, Canada, Australia, New Zealand and
> the Irish Free State, they take some managing don't they? No
> politics ever introduced in the British Empire caused me so much
> trouble as this damn bodyline bowling!
> All I can say is don't take Larwood with you to Canada!

He had assumed that he would not be quoted in the press. When Harold Larwood raised the remarks in a Sunday newspaper Thomas tried to deny having made them, but reports of his short speech had been printed in *The Times*, the *Daily Telegraph* and the *Evening Standard*.

The MCC declined to comment on the Downing Street meeting but from a letter Findlay wrote to Viscount Ullswater it is clear that the conference with Thomas at the Dominions Office precipitated a decision to call a meeting of the Committee. Findlay continued: 'After the meeting at the Dominions Office the President and other members of the Committee who attended felt that it was desirable to communicate again with the Australian Board of Control.' The Dominions Office was beginning to give a political direction to the MCC Committee in the same way as the Lyons government in Australia was feeling the need to exert pressure on the Board of Control. The bodyline cricket crisis had become an issue of imperial diplomatic importance.

Findlay made a series of hurried phone calls to ensure the fullest attendance of the Committee. They met at Lord's, rather than the usual Junior Carlton Club, for two hours on Thursday 2 February. The outcome was two more telegrams. The first to the Board included a direct and very specific question: 'May we accept this as a clear indication that the good sportsmanship of our team is not in question?' The Australian Board were faced with a clear choice. Either they could maintain their position that bodyline bowling was unsportsmanlike and risk the tour being cancelled, or back down. The Australian government was exerting considerable pressure for them to adopt the latter course.

The second telegram was from Findlay to Warner: 'Circumstances make it impossible to defer reply to Board. We hope cable we are sending will facilitate your negotiations. Please inform Jardine.' Warner's peacemaking efforts centred on a statement that he had drafted which he hoped would reassure public opinion of good faith on both sides before the fourth test began. This solemn affirmation was to be signed by Jardine, Palairet and Warner on behalf of the MCC and by Woodfull and Robertson, the Chairman of the Australian Board. It read:

> The game of cricket is so great that it will survive any storm that may centre around it. There has unfortunately been such a storm but let us all put that behind us and start afresh in the spirit of good sportsmanship which has characterised the matches between England and Australia for the past seventy years. We look forward confidently to a very happy fourth test match at Brisbane and sincerely hope for the cooperation of the public on whose good will and good temper so much depends. Let everyone of us remember that we come from the same stock and that cricket and its traditions are part of our common heritage.

While it appealed to the imperial heritage and cricket's traditions it did nothing to tackle the crucial issues which were at the centre of the controversy. Would England use bodyline in the Brisbane test? And would the Australian Board withdraw the accusation of 'unsportsmanlike' behaviour?

The Australians were certain that Jardine would refuse to sign this public statement. They were quite correct. In his tour book, *In Quest of the Ashes*, Jardine dismisses the proposed text as being 'admirable' but 'pious'. There might be a time for devout and righteous comments but for Jardine this was not the moment. He wanted a retraction of the word unsportsmanlike and nothing else was acceptable.

London had done everything it could. Crutchley, while talking to the Board's delegates in Sydney and to Joe Lyons, the Australian Prime Minister, kept the Dominions Office appraised of his movements. He sent London a secret telegram to inform them that he would be in Sydney from 6 to 8 February. The cable which saved the fourth test and the tour was sent by the Board on 8 February, and reassured Lord's that 'We do not regard the sportsmanship of your term as being in question'.

For the most part, British press coverage of the Adelaide test and the bodyline controversy supported Jardine and the MCC, and denounced the Australians as 'squealers'. The pro-Labour *Daily Herald*, in an editional on 19 January, urged that there should be 'no sentimental climbdown' and pressed the MCC 'to let him [Jardine] lead'. The first person in the British newspapers to object to the England tactics was Neville Cardus. As early as 8 January he had written in the *Observer*: 'I hope we have heard the last of leg theory violence'. On 16 January, during the Adelaide test, his comments in the *Guardian* took on a stronger tone: 'It is brutal . . . the morality of such bowling is open to question . . . Frankly, it does not seem cricket to me.' The following day he continued; 'This violence which is essentially against the spirit of cricket must be stopped . . . The primary aim of fast leg theory bowling is intimidation.' In February he expressed his thoughts about Jardine's captaincy in the *Observer*. Jardine's philosophy was to 'knock the man down first and be compassionate afterwards', and Jardine was 'the dour exponent of realpolitik in cricket'.

By this time Cardus was not alone in voicing reservations about the England tactics. He was joined by a number of well-known former England players. Ranjitsinhji: 'I disapprove strongly of a concerted leg side attack, if it is existent. I would rather lose the rubber than win over bruised bodies of my opponents.' Archie MacLaren: 'There is nothing to recommend this pounding of the body throughout an innings because eventually the batsman will be seriously hurt.' Arthur Gilligan: 'Cricket is supposed to be fair and this does not savour of it in the slightest.'

Here were the views of two former England captains and one of the greatest batsmen ever to represent England. Their opinions were formed in England and in India from less material than was available to the MCC Committee at Lord's, but they quickly condemned bodyline bowling. To excuse the MCC because of poor communications and misinformation, as is now common practice, is to cover up and white-wash their abject failure.

Archie MacLaren, who Neville Cardus considers taught him 'the meaning of epic romance, style, generosity of gesture', made his feelings on bodyline clear to the Committee in private as well. He informed Findlay that the Committee had no right to reply to the Board's telegram on the basis that 'we', the members, are 'MCC'. Findlay commented to Lacey on 28 January that MacLaren was being 'difficult'. The Committee had probably come to expect this sort of behaviour from Archie, who despite having captained England 22 times against Australia had gained a reputation for being emotionally unpredictable.

The support for Jardine and his methods mounted after the victory in the fourth test which regained England the Ashes. On 15 February the MCC sent Jardine a telegram which read: 'Well done carry on the good work', and another to Harold Larwood: 'Well bowled. Congratulations'. Viscount Lewisham sent a personal message to Jardine on 16 February: 'Splendid, well played all. My heartiest congratulations'. King George V despatched a cable via Viscount Lewisham and Lord's as follows:

> As patron of the MCC I wish you to convey to the team in
> Australia my warm congratulations on their victory. I have
> followed with the closest interest the ups and downs of the last
> match.
> George R.I.

The phrase 'ups and downs' was a little unfortunate in the circumstances, but King George V had a reputation for enjoying an amusing story. The King would have been kept informed of the cricketing events by his Private Secretary, Sir Clive Wigram, a longtime member of the MCC who had been in touch with Findlay after the defeat in the second test in Melbourne and expressed his disappointment at the loss.

Ramsay MacDonald, the Prime Minister, sent a simple message of congratulations while J.H. Thomas sent a euphoric cable: 'Bravo, the Ashes are won. But they are secondary to the great fighting spirit and good sportsmanship shown by both sides.' The choice of words is again dubious, reinforcing the view from London that there was no question of 'unsportsmanlike' behaviour. In Australia the 'good sportsmanship' of the England captain and his bodyline bowling tactics were still very much in doubt.

As the dust began to settle the *New Statesman* ran a poem by their regular lyrical columnist, MacFlecknoe. In light-hearted and jocular vein this draws the connections between cricket, politics and Empire:

Some folks seem to be astonished, but doesn't startle me
To discover Jimmie Thomas chatting with the MCC;
For an empire-builder's duty is by any means to seek
Fresh and up-to-date improvements in Imperial technique

Now we know that Larwood's bowling may affect the fate of
   nations,
And that leg-traps may imperil our Imperial relations,
He, our master hand at bargains, must be hungering to wield
All the diplomatic assets lurking in the cricket field.

Dimly one can see the process—say the British exports fall:
'If you'll give us further preference, Larwood shall not bowl at all'
While if meat should be in question, then experience suggests
An increased quota, in return for four day Tests.

But while thus employing cricket to cement the Commonwealth,
We shall make it clear that Britons don't play cricket for their health;
If the Test Match should be cancelled, we shall tax at higher rate
All Australia has to send us, to recoup the vanished 'gate'.

So the weapons that have banished unemployment from our land
And impressed the Irish voter with the weight of Britain's hand
Shall be sharpened and perfected—that is how it seems to me—
By the aid of Jimmie Thomas and the MCC.

5
Political consequences in Australia

That first hasty telegram, sent to London from Adelaide on 18 January 1933 in the immediate aftermath of the row raised at Oldfield's injury, touched off a series of political chain reactions which carried the controversy well beyond Adelaide's boundary fences. The first level of reaction involved relations between the Australian players and their governing body. In turn, that helped unmask divisions within the Australian Cricket Board itself. The resultant uncertain handling of the crisis allowed the English team management to enlist the support of its local political representative who ushered the matter into the realms of official Anglo-Australian relations bureaucracy. Inevitably, the issue went from there to British political circles. This process was fanned by the ongoing fragility of wider Anglo-Australian relations and the consistently fierce protest of the Australian press which aggravated the Australian public's response to the new English cricket tactics.

The starting point lies with the members of the Australian Cricket Board of Control which, by the 1930s, was still heir to the squabbles, suspicions and jealousies to which it was born. Like the political federation movement which led to the Australian Commonwealth, the creation of the Board had been a frustrating affair. As the most populous states, Victoria and New South Wales had dominated Australia's early cricketing government. English tours were underwritten first by the Melbourne Cricket Club as the premier cricket body, but by the 1890s the Sydney Cricket Ground trustees were also involved.

Two basic problems bedevilled early attempts to form a national body. The power of the Melbourne Cricket Club was not universally welcomed in Victoria's cricket community, and the New South Wales Cricket Association considered other state bodies less fitted than itself for the task of control. Nevertheless, the Board was established in 1905 with the Melbourne Cricket Club receiving special preference in Victoria. Queensland joined the two founder states shortly after the creation of the Board. South Australia entered in 1906, Tasmania in 1908, and Western Australia a few years later. Once the full Board was established the representation quota was set at three members each from New South Wales, Victoria and South Australia, two from Queensland, and one each from Tasmania and Western Australia.

From its earliest days the Board was a controversial institution, with what many in the states regarded as its unwarranted accumulation of power lying at the heart of the problem. Just like the federal government system, the Board was widely regarded (rightly or wrongly) to step on individual and states' rights far too keenly. The 1912 tour affair set the tone for much of the Board's subsequent unpopularity.

Australian touring teams traditionally had chosen their own managers and when the Board was established the practice continued, the Board retaining the right to confirm the players' choice. For the 1909 tour of England, however, the Board appointed the vice-captain also as treasurer to 'assist' the players' choice of Frank Laver as manager. Once the tour finished, a fierce and public quarrel broke out between Laver and the Board, the manager maintaining that some of the information sought from him should be gathered more properly from the treasurer. As the time approached for the 1912 tour to England, the dispute spilled over into pamphleteering, complete with newspaper charges and countercharges of either criminal activity in the financial area or victimisation based on personal prejudice, depending on the source of the allegation. The Board indicated that it would hold increased power over managerial appointments, and several leading players protested about an imposition on their rights. Public meetings were held, some chaired by the Premier of New South Wales, and extreme accusations were levelled by each side. The upshot was that the touring party proceeded to England without six of Australia's most famous cricketing names: Clem Hill, Warwick Armstrong, Victor Trumper, Vernon Ransford, Tibby Cotter and Hanson Carter. This made the Board widely unpopular.

Subsequent disputes never reached the heights of the 1912 fiasco, but there were frequent mutterings in cricket circles, and occasionally outside them, about Board inadequacies. Players' rights were thought to be eroded constantly, and the composition of the Board was considered overly conservative and restricted, given that membership depended more upon a powerbase in state organisations than upon an experience of cricket at a high competitive level. These feelings meant that Board actions often suffered public rebuke, especially in 1930 when Don Bradman, having scored the best-ever test series average and aggregate, was fined by the Board for writing about his experience. It was such arbitrary actions which gave the Board such a weak public relations image. Largely because of the Bradman issue Mr H.R.R. Grieve, a Member of the Legislative Council of New South Wales, early in 1933 publicly branded the Board as on oligarchy responsible to no-one and lamented its 'assumption of power incompatible with the prosperity of Australian cricket'.

The thirteen person Board at the time of bodyline shared a common social heritage, an average education, and a commerical-professional background. One of the New South Wales members, for example, traced his ancestry to an infantry officer of the New South Wales Regiment who arrived at Sydney in 1792. Similarly, the Western Australian representative descended from families that had been among that state's early colonists. At least half of the members had been educated at prestigious private schools, and many had proceeded to a university education, particularly for the professions—there were at least four lawyers and two medical practitioners among them. There were, besides, two stock exchange members, a pastoral agent, the managing director of a timber company, and a bread company director. Their membership of the Board invariably followed a lengthy spell in state cricket administration, where their positions in some part resulted from their social and occupational status. Some individual examples of Board membership confirm this overall picture.

The Chairman of the Board, Allen William David Robertson, demonstrated the power of cricket as a vehicle for upward social mobility and public respectability. Born in 1867 in Deniliquin, on the Victoria-New South Wales border, where his father ran a general store, he was orphaned at an early age and went to Melbourne in the care of an aunt. He worked first in a warehouse and was then apprenticed to a chemist for whom he worked in a number of Victorian country towns. During his time in the country, Robertson qualified for entrance to the University of Melbourne, where he began studying medicine part-time, eventually graduating at 36. He worked in private practice in Melbourne besides holding various hospital posts. Capitalising on his professional standing, he formed a business partnership with other doctors and developed property in the heart of Melbourne. The social mobility which augmented this economic success stemmed from his involvement with the University Cricket Club. Robertson was appointed as its president in 1914; five years later he became a Victorian representative on the Board of Control, and its chairman in 1930.

William Charles Bull, a New South Wales representative, sprang from a more established social position. His great-grandfathers had arrived as soldiers during the first twelve years of the colony's life. His father was born in Liverpool, New South Wales, and into a family trained to the legal profession, a promising avenue towards colonial social acceptance. (The pattern was similar to that set during a similar period by Gubby Allen's forebears.) A sporting and professional background led into local government, with mayoralty of Liverpool and Hurstville, then into the state's Legislative Assembly as member for Camden during the 1890s. William Charles Bull was born in 1881 (one of eleven children), educated at Sydney Grammar, admitted to the bar in 1909, and joined his uncle's practice. He quickly became a prominent member of the New South Wales Cricket Association, becoming an Australian Board of Control member in 1925 and managing a touring party to New Zealand in 1928.

Frank Maitland Cush, from New South Wales, was born in 1893 and helped run the family business, a timber outlet with interests in box and case manufacture. From this he branched into civic work, such as serving on the Board of Directors of the St George District Hospital. His rise to the Board was rapid, coming in 1930 just three years after his election to the New South Wales Cricket Association executive.

Robert Aubrey Oxlade was the remaining New South Wales member. A shadowy figure to the public at large, he was to prove one of the key figures in the Board's handling of the bodyline crisis. Another lawyer, Oxlade's rise to the Board was from his Manly club base to the New South Wales Cricket Association.

The two Queensland members revealed slightly different backgrounds. Roger Joseph Hartigan was born in Sydney during 1879, the son of migrant Irish parents. Educated at the Christian Brothers, Lewisham, in 1895 he joined the New Zealand Loan Company as a junior clerk. By the time he shifted to Brisbane in 1905 he had played cricket and baseball for New South Wales. His sports career flourished in Queensland where he played state cricket and lacrosse. in 1907–08 he played two tests for Australia, joining the select band to make a century in his first test and then toured England in 1909. His business career flourished when in 1921 he became departmental manager and wool auctioneer for the Queensland Primary Producers' Cooperative. Meanwhile, his administrative work led to membership of the Board.

John Silvester Hutcheon was born in 1882 and educated at Toowoomba Grammer School before going to England and being admitted as a lawyer to Lincolns Inn. Returning to Brisbane he represented the state at cricket, including a spell as captain; played tennis for Brisbane; and was selected for Australia at Lacrosse, which at that time was especially popular among the professional middle-class and its aspiring members. Hutcheon became a Board member in 1919, beginning a term which was to last almost 40 years and included a spell as chairman in 1924–25.

Henry Warburton Hodgetts, from Adelaide, was born in 1882 and educated at the prestigious St Peters College before joining the Commonwealth Public Service in Adelaide attached to the Postmaster General's Department. After twelve years there he spent six as secretary to the Adelaide Stock Exchange, before founding his own broking business. (the one to which he would attract Don Bradman in the mid-1930s) In the late 1930s, he went to prison for misappropriation of company funds.

Roy Foster Middleton, Hodgett's co-member from Adelaide, played for South Australia before the First World War, and spent most of his adult life on the state's Cricket Association. He, too, moved in business circles, becoming manager of the Executor Trustees and Agency Company of South Australia.

The Western Australia delegate was Samuel Harold Drew Rowe, one of his state's earliest fine players with a good record against touring sides. He was educated at the turn of the century at Hale, already a leading private school; married the daughter of a bakery business proprietor; became secretary-manager to a business company based on those family interests; and also became Chairman of Directors of a flourmilling concern. He was one of Perth cricket's most influential figures and his elevation to the Board was almost inevitable.

When bodyline arrived these men were part of an institution with a short but turbulent and divided history. Given communication difficulties—telegraph rather than telephone was still the rule—they did not see or keep in touch with each other on a regular basis and some even used proxies at the few full Board meetings held. It was virtually impossible to get them all together at short notice to meet any serious crisis, and that was to have considerable impact upon their handling of bodyline. While they were certainly solid citizens, few if any were in positions of great public or political significance—and certainly not in the way MCC Committee members were. Put simply, they were not practiced in the ways of handling publicly delicate matters which spread beyond the cricket field. They were in a position of learning rather than manipulating. On the other hand, their backgrounds ensured that their attitudes towards the etiquette of cricket were informed thoroughly by English practice. The private schools which many of them attended were staffed liberally by men with an English public school and university heritage. That bodyline tactics came from an English side made the handling of them that much more difficult for the Board.

From the outset of the tour the Board was in difficulty on two fronts. The first concerned the distinct possibility that, because of Board policy, Don Bradman would take no part in the series. After his fracas with the Board in 1930 Bradman had signed a contract to both write about and broadcast on the test matches. He duly applied to the Board for permission and was refused, although Jack Fingleton, more a journalist than Bradman in the professional sense, was granted permission. Bradman announced that if he could not write he would not play in the tests. The public outcry was immediate and uncomplimentary to the Board. That Bradman was able to play was solely due to his newspaper bosses releasing him from his obligations. Key figures in the release were Sir Hugh Denison and R.C. Packer, then Managing Editor of Associated Press. (His grandson Kerry became architect of the World Series Cricket revolution in 1977.)

Denison, Chairman of Associated Newspapers which ran both the *Sun* (for which Bradman was to write) and the *Daily Telegraph*, was educated at top-line private schools: Scotch College, Melbourne and Prince Alfred, Adelaide. He then went on to University College, London, before returning for a brief spell in the South Australian parliament between 1901 and 1905. He was, therefore, connected to the Adelaide social circles which were to initiate official intervention in bodyline. Denison's Anglophile background was extended when he shifted to Sydney where he was a prime mover in founding a branch of the British Empire Society. It is not difficult to see why, Denison waived his company's hold on Bradman to enable Australia's premier batsman to play in the most important imperial sporting competition.

However, Denison's action did not end the matter of public comment by participating players. During the first test it became clear that cricket broadcasting was growing more popular and radio stations wanted players' comments. At the end of each day's play, cricketers gave their view on what had happened on rival stations. At the Board meeting held near the end of December, a Victorian member moved a prohibition of player broadcasts pending a full review at the end of the season. At the same time an amendment to the player-writer rule was defeated, with five members supporting the unsuccessful move. This divided opinion, though largely masked from public view, characterised the Board's attempts to handle bodyline and created an internal power struggle. It also had a direct impact upon the players' attempts to convince the Board to find some solution.

The initial telegram was sent from Adelaide to London on 18 January 1933, the afternoon before the match concluded. It was drafted by four Board members. Hodgetts, Middleton and B.V. Scrymgour from South Australia, and W.L. Kelly from Victoria. According to a subsequent inquiry within the Board, another four members approved the draft: Bushby from Tasmania, Rowe, Mailer from Victoria and his chairman-colleague Robertson. It is equally clear that the other five—New South Wales and Queensland *en bloc*—were very worried by the wording, considered they had been consulted insufficiently if at all, and said so vigorously when the MCC replied. Leader of the dissenting side was Aubrey Oxlade.

Those Board members in Adelaide were subjected to enormous pressure both by public reaction to events and by demands from players that something be done. Woodfull took the lead for his men. His best-known utterance at Adelaide was to Warner when the English manager visited the Australian dressing-room to commiserate on the Australian captain's injuries. Woodfull noted that of two teams in the game, only one was playing 'cricket'. But Woodfull also made his feelings clear to

William Woodfull

the Board members. As a letter he wrote to the Board at the time explained, he was not concerned simply for the damage to his players: 'Since entering Test cricket I have not been sure that it is for the good of the Empire that in times when England and Australia need to be pulling together large sections of both countries are embittered.' His manual on cricket was to reveal a sound belief in the moral good of English cricket tradition, but here he was thinking that the entire future of the game was in jeopardy as a result of actions taken by the supreme cricketing power.

The players themselves were not in agreement about what should be done. Vic Richardson in his autobiography, for example, later claimed that he opposed the sending of the cable. He thought the series should be played out, then a secret report sent to London detailing the English iniquities. Several players thought retaliation in kind the most viable response, though against this were the lack of adequate firepower at Australia's disposal and Woodfull's opposition, in which he was supported by many eminent Australian cricket authorities.

The Australian camp was in some disarray, then, and the Board's internal struggle did nothing to strengthen the hand against a very organised MCC. Meanwhile, the issue had begun to pass beyond the Board's immediate control. As many contemporary and later reports confirm, all sections of the Adelaide crowd were incensed by what they saw happening. Bill O'Reilly, who played in the match, and his biographer R.S. Whitington, who was in the members' stand, both recalled the fury of that day: 'those octogenarian Adam's apples throbbing above the starched white collars of respected Adelaide Oval members . . . standing in line between the tiered pavilion seats . . . hooting and counting the Englishmen out'. Like the members' stand on any Australian ground, that in Adelaide contained the cream of local society, at least some of whom were not prepared to let the matter rest there.

Sir Walter Young, for example, was then about 60 and head of Elder Smith, one of Australia's premier rural traders. Given the importance of rural produce in Australia's economy, the discussions at imperial level about the future of primary trade, and the impact upon it of the economic depression, men like Young had considerable influence in federal and imperial circles. In fact, Young's 1928 knighthood followed much 1920s work on imperial trade and finance matters.

Young's membership of the exclusive Adelaide Club, and his general commercial importance, put him in touch with most of Adelaide's leading men. These included Sir Wallace Bruce, a major industrial and commercial figure who had served as Adelaide's Lord Mayor in 1925–27. He was national chairman for the Chambers of Commerce in the mid 1920s, and in 1930 chaired the federal committee enquiring into the Economic Problem, as it was known.

J.G. Duncan-Hughes also played a key role. Born in 1882 he was the eldest son of Sir John Duncan, state politician, landholder and prominent early colonial figure. Duncan-Hughes attended Cheltenham Grammar, St Peters College and Trinity College where he graduated in law. After a few years at the bar, and a distinguished war during which he won the Military Cross, he joined federal parliament in 1922 until his defeat in 1928. He returned to Canberra as a senator in 1931. He married into a family related to Sir Edwin Smith, Adelaide's most notable early civic figure. Active in cricket and athletic circles, Duncan-Hughes was also a member of such diverse groups as the state's Caledonian Society and Orpheus Society. Interests in mining and property broadened his network. One telling connection lay in the South Australian Institution for the Blind, Deaf and Dumb—he had served on its committee with B.V. Scrymgour, the South Australian representative on the Board of Control and one of those who drafted the first telegram.

As if that were not enough Duncan-Hughes's brother, Sir Walter Duncan, was also involved. A pastoralist, he was elected to the state's Legislative Council in 1918 and was on very good terms with a succession of governors, including Hore-Ruthven. Along with his brother, he was a leading light in the Adelaide Club, which was an appropriate venue for their Liberal and Country Party political affiliations.

F.L. Dumas has been mentioned, principally by Laurence Le Quesne in *The Bodyline Controversy*, as a central Adelaide figure, but he was not so powerfully influential as these others. Born in 1890, the son of the *Mount Barker Courier* proprietor, Dumas joined the *Advertiser* in 1907, then went to the *Argus* in Melbourne. During the conscription debate of the First World War Dumas travelled with Prime Minister Billy Hughes. He then became chief editor at the *Argus*. In 1929 he returned to Adelaide to become managing editor of the *Advertiser*. Socially he in no way matched the Duncan group but he had one great strength—he held sway over Adelaide's major avenue for influencing public opinion.

This tightknit group of Adelaide figures possessed enormous power and influence in political, social and economic circles. Once they interested themselves in the affairs of bodyline, there were bound to be widespread repercussions. Young and his like-minded colleagues clearly expressed their views to the cricket authorities themselves, principally to W.H. (Bill) Jeanes, a Glenelg real estate agent and Justice of the Peace who was secretary to both the South Australian Cricket Association and the Australian Board. Tim Wall, the South Australian fast bowler who was at the other end when Oldfield was hit, recalled in an interview many years later that Jeanes was 'a bit pompous' and not overly popular with the players. Nevertheless, Jeanes was in the thick of things during the composition of the first cable.

The Young group soon sought redress elsewhere, as the South Australian Governor's office diary reveals. The diary, now held in the South Australian State Archives, was almost certainly kept by Cyril Legh Winser, private secretary to a succession of governors in the state and himself an accomplished sportsman. He had won the Australian amateur golf championship and the South Australian title many times, and in his cricketing days kept wicket to the great English bowler Sydney Barnes during his Staffordshire days. Winser later handed to Lord's a collection of official and semi-official documents relating to bodyline and its resolution, particularly concerning the role of Sir Alexander Hore-Ruthven. So far, that collection has not been made available for research purposes.

The diary kept by Winser documents a number of critical meetings which helped propel the bodyline issue into official political circles. On 11 January 1933, before the test, an official dinner was hosted at the Adelaide Club by the Lieutenant-Governor, G.J.R. Murray (Hore-Ruthven being on leave in England). Murray was yet another powerful Adelaide establishment figure with a strong affection for things English. Born in 1863 into a founding pastoralist family he took the St Peters route to Adelaide University then Trinity College, Cambridge. He was admitted to the Inner Temple in London in 1888 before returning to the South Australian legal profession. In 1906 he became a King's Counsel, and in 1912 was elevated to the state's Supreme Court. Just four years later he became both Chief Justice and Lieutenant-

Governor, posts he retained in the bodyline season. The dinner guests of 11 January included Warner, Palairet, Jardine, Sir Walter Duncan and several other prominent citizens.

On 16 January, the day Oldfield was hit, Sir Walter Young hosted another dinner for the English visitors and there was 'much talk about the cricket incidents'. The following day, 'Warner came to see Lt. Gov. & discuss situation'. On the day after that, the first Board telegram was sent off.

At this very early point, then, Warner had raised the cricketing issue with the acting representative of the Crown in South Australia, surely in the hope that discussion of at least an informal kind would arise further up the chain of official command, and knowing that a major row was in the offing. The fair conclusion might be that he felt unconfident of containing that row himself and in need of additional support. By taking the matter outside cricket circles Warner perhaps hoped to gain added leverage against his captain. This early move towards official contact coincided with the Board's frantic attempts within the Australian cricketing world to put together, get support for and despatch its telegram.

Meanwhile public opinion remained heated, stimulated by the unprecedented press coverage. During the Melbourne test, for example, Don Bradman spoke about his views of the match on radio 3DB, creating enormous attention—not the least because he criticised the performances of some fellow players. Radio 2UW in Sydney later established a radiotelephone hookup with stations in Melbourne and Adelaide so that people like A.E.R. Gilligan (1924-25 MCC tour captain now turned commentator) and E.P. Barbour (medical practitioner, ex-New South Wales player, administrator and *Sydney Morning Herald* columnist) might share their views with the thousands of listeners. That was on the very night the Board sent off its first salvo. Papers like the *West Australian* declared that it would not be sorry to bid farewell to a man such as Jardine who had besmirched the game. The Melbourne *Argus*, which provided sobering views on the whole matter, thought that good tempers and senses of humour were being overridden by the 'expert' commentary which took the nation right into the dressing rooms. One correspondent to the *Bulletin* tried to warn that the mass of 'pestilent rubbish' touted about was aggravating the situation. Some papers printed reports that the touring party was split over Jardine's methods, captaincy and non-selection of Maurice Tate—a team statement subsequently denied this.

Initial Australian press reaction to the first telegram was divided— some saw it as dignified and reasonable whereas for others it was hasty and hysterical. Some changed their views as the 'success' of the cable ebbed and flowed. Additional pressure was building upon the Board from state cricket associations. On 25 January, for example, the New South Wales Executive urged that the tour must be completed. Such pressure limited the options available to the Board, reducing its bargaining power as the English counter-offensive mounted.

Within Adelaide political circles the telegram was clearly seen as not entirely successful. It was known that Warner and Palairet had discussed the matter with those Board members available in Adelaide prior to the sending of the cable. The local version of those discussions was that the English managers claimed tactics were the sole province of the captain. On the English side, Warner argued that he had begged for the telegram not to be sent in that form. The local establishment decided upon a new initiative.

Walter Duncan and some other notables consulted the Lt-Governor, suggesting he send a telegram to inform Hore-Ruthven in London about the state of play. Legh Winser, sensing that such a move would pitch matters squarely into official registered form, suggested a softer manouevre. He persuaded Young and Duncan-Hughes to send a cable to the Governor in their private capacities, probably the first non-media communication Hore-Ruthven received from Australia. That was on 24 January 1933.

Part of Winser's caution almost certainly stemmed from the fact that a British official touring Australia in his capacity as a senior officer in the Bank of England was about to arrive in Adelaide for talks. Any unduly strident reaction to bodyline might have upset the balance of those discussions, especially as the English press was generally dismissing Australian reactions as over-sensitive. This explanation is supported by the fact that Winser called Young in personally on 25 January to prepare for the financial meeting.

Yet this caution could not halt the flow of events and the establishment's desire to blunt the English attack. The next day the Lt-

Robert Aubrey Oxlade

Governor sent the first official political telegram to Hore-Ruthven that set in train the first strand of the London official actions already discussed in Chapter Four.

It is worth reflecting again on the magnitude of these incidents. Events on a cricket field had been deemed so prejudicial to imperial goodwill that influential Australians, mostly Anglophile, had sought official intervention from British government authorities. This was an unprecedented request, creating probably the first modern 'sport and politics' crisis. It also opened up parallel lines of official political discussion. This was a South Australian request, no doubt sought in the national interest, via the local British representative. The British federal representative was also about to become involved.

Public reaction was beginning to show divisions when the MCC's reply was received, basically daring the Australian authorities to take responsibility for an unthinkable tour cancellation. At a public reception in Ballarat, the acting Mayor expressed the hope that Australian players would not stoop to the brute force of English methods. On the other hand, the *Bulletin* castigated the Board for its 'hysterical protest' which had placed Australia in such an awkward position: 'what hurts most is that Australians who have no use for the board or its works may be mistaken for small-minded people who attach exaggerated importance to cricket matches and can't win without skiting or lose without squealing'. The *Sydney Morning Herald* took a similar if softer line, requesting saner considerations from the Board if only to confirm its local authority.

The Board's divisions began to emerge publicly just prior to a special meeting called to discuss the position. On 25 January Harold Rowe, who had supported the initial telegram, was quoted in eastern newspapers as saying that England had played within the cricket laws, that the protest should have been sent at the conclusion of the tour, and that he hoped the Board's special meeting would do nothing 'hysterical'. As if to underline that, it was announced on 28 January that Rowe would be represented at that special meeting by a proxy, George Miles, the state politician who made a 'cricket and Empire' speech at the first public reception of the tour. Miles was also senior vice-president of the Western Australian Cricket Association, which had made it very clear that it would not support a cancellation of the tour and did not favour retaliation by Australian bowlers.

Plum Warner, meanwhile, was moving in in a different direction. On 27 January 1933 he wrote from Sydney to his personal friend and Britain's official representative in Australia, E.T. Crutchley, in Canberra. It was in response to an inquiry from Crutchley seeking, as he put it in his diary, 'the truth about the Adelaide fracas'. Warner described the closing of the Adelaide ground during practice because of Jardine's dissatisfaction about spectator behaviour. He went on:

> The Board of Control's telegram was silly, tactless and rude...MCC's reply was superb. The Board must withdraw the word 'unsportsmanlike' and then the situation will be quite easy...I am very hopeful that the great commonsense of the British people will very shortly put things right, but the Board here certainly need a new draughtsman.

The battle between the committees had entered another phase: it was no longer a question of simple tactics but almost of morality. The English team could not continue under any suspicion that they were 'unsportsmanlike'. Throughout the Empire 'playing the game' was a moral code, and cricket itself would be eroded if the slur was allowed to remain. Warner's comments, coming just before the Board's special meeting, put Crutchley on the alert. The two men, of course, were well known to each other. They had travelled out to Australia on the same boat. They became firm friends, and their sons were to live next to each other many years later.

Ernest Tristram Crutchley was not the typical British representative overseas, nor even a typical high-level civil servant. Born in 1878 the son of a Royal Navy commander, he had worked his way up from the bottom. His education was undistinguished and non-university. Just prior to the war he reached the rank of Assistant Surveyor in the British Post Office. During the war he served with the engineers, demobilising as a lieutenant-colonel. Like Duncan-Hughes and Hore-Ruthven, he served with distinction at Gallipoli. Service on the staff of the Chief Secretary for Ireland then led Crutchley into the Dominions Office. There he reached Assistant Secretary, mostly in the Overseas Settlement Department, before being seconded to Australia first as British Migration Representative then, from 1931, as Official Representative of the British Government in Australia.

Crutchley's stay in Australia was personally and professionally difficult. He arrived in Canberra in its very young days and found it a most unpleasant place in which to live. Although he developed good contacts, he found it almost impossible to get into 'good clubs' despite his political status. His relationships with the governors were undefined, making his status unclear and his position none the more tenable. Politically his time coincided with a potentially explosive Anglo-Australian relationship. Consequently he was most sensitive to any potential irritant. During the bodyline period, for example, he wrote to London fearing that the New South Wales and Victorian Labor parties were being taken over by radicals based in the Sydney and Melbourne universities. On bodyline itself he pushed the English position to the hilt, but made it very clear to Warner that he abhorred the new tactics. A determined and competent man, he was also a skilful negotiator who believed strongly in the bonds of Empire. This is conveyed in a speech he gave in Canberra during 1931, about the time of his appointment as official representative:

> I have myself also always visualised the need for this connecting link, not only for what I may call business reasons, but for psychological reasons, to keep each nation informed of what is happening in the other, to interpret national aspirations and the national mind of one to the other, and to secure in some desirable respects a greater tendency towards uniformity of thought.

Crutchley would have been acutely aware of bodyline's potential for damaging the psychological and practical links between Britain and Australia, not to mention its working against 'uniformity of thought'.

The Board of Control met on 30 January 1933 in what the *Sydney Morning Herald* understatedly called a 'serious mood' and the London *Observer* predicted would be an attempt to 'climb out of the grave which it has dug for itself'. It tried to exclude its deliberations from public comment but a number of people must have been prepared to talk, because newspapers reported a fairly accurate view of the power struggle which is now evident in the terse minutes of the meeting. The Queensland and New South Wales delegates were clearly angry that actions had been taken on their behalf without adequate consultation. Hutcheon and Hartigan had written to Jeanes specifically opposing the action. They were aggravated further that matters had been dominated by South Australian delegates whom they regarded as minor figures.

During the all-day bargaining a sub-committee of review was established with forces equally represented: Middleton and Scrymgour from South Australia, Oxlade and Hutcheon from New South Wales and Queensland. Robertson was also on it in his capacity as Board Chairman, but his influence was somewhat offset by Hutcheon being given the chair of the sub-committee.

At the end of the meeting Robertson released a statement claiming that in a very fruitful meeting there had been no dissension, and that all those not present in Adelaide were fully satisfied with the actions on their behalf. This was most clearly not the case, as became clear at a full Board meeting held some time later. Oxlade asked that a series of questions he had raised at the special meeting, and which had been omitted from the minutes, be written into the records: (1) how many delegates had supported the Adelaide telegram? (2) who had drafted the cable? (3) at what time had that cable been sent? (4) what were the circumstances leading to the despatch?

The special meeting, then, was held in a climate of some heat with the opposed factions struggling for control over the handling of the controversy. Robertson, in particular, was feeling the pressure. By all accounts he was not so strongwilled as Oxlade who had taken leadership of the dissident group. The numbers held for Robertson, eight to five as on the earlier occasion, but he was in the weaker position in the long term. Rowe had already revealed publicly his doubts about the Board's position and if just one other delegate broke ranks and it came to a vote of confidence, Robertson might find himself in the minority. He had foreseen this—before the meeting he kept in close touch with Jeanes, his secretary, complaining about the opposition forces. That was as much a hint to the South Australian delegates, through Jeanes, to hold firm as it was recrimination of the dissenters.

Given this divided background, and its tinges of bitterness and temper, it was not surprising that the more careful reconsideration sought by Plum Warner and others did not eventuate. The Board certainly retreated from its first position, but while it tried to repair damage caused in the first phase it did nothing to repair any which resulted at the second level from the use of 'unsportsmanlike'. Its new cable to the MCC did not mention the word. Rather, it suggested the English body was in an awkward position trying to deal with the issue in London where it had not even seen the type of bowling in question.

Political consequences in Australia

The Board repeated its view that bodyline endangered both players and the spirit of the game. It did not consider cancellation of the tour was necessary.

Days earlier Warner had emphasised in his letter to Crutchley how important it was that the word be withdrawn. On 3 February the *Argus*, in its usually sensible way, argued editorially for the word's deletion. It had heard that the matter was now in diplomatic circles where concern for the niceties of address might lead to an exchange of official notes, and thought there would be laughter among amused and bewildered foreigners. It was certainly right in at least one respect—the matter had reached official diplomatic level.

When the Board released its reply to MCC, Warner sent this telegram which Crutchley received on 1 February:

Have under consideration cancellation of remaining matches of tour including test owing to failure of Board to remove stigma of word unsportsmanlike in their first cable. Beg you use your influence to get word withdrawn. Matter very urgent.

The urgency almost certainly concerned what amounted to a strike among MCC players until the attack on their characters was removed. Unfortunately for Warner, he sent the telegram uncoded. A clerk, presumably with partisan cricket interests, leaked the contents to a member of the press. This happened so quickly that within minutes of receiving the telegram Crutchley was being questioned on its implications by a Canberra representative of Associated Press, and within a day rumours and reports were circulating widely about very high-level political involvement in the affair.

As soon as he received Warner's telegram, Crutchley telephoned Prime Minister Joe Lyons in Melbourne whose opening comment, according to Crutchley's diary, was: 'it looks as though we are leading two opposing armies'. Crutchley outlined the situation as he saw it, and Lyons 'agreed that the cancellation of the tour would be a very grave thing, for Australia especially, just when feeling was so good'. Crutchley sought a withdrawal of the word unsportsmanlike, and Lyons countered with an inquiry about what the touring team was prepared to offer as a conciliatory gesture—he most likely asked for a modification to the bodyline tactics. Although Crutchley had no authority to do so, he told Lyons that a modification to the field placings might be possible. Lyons agreed to contact Robertson, chairman of the Board, who was also in Melbourne.

There is a possibility that Lyons had been involved already. A week earlier the London *Daily Herald* had claimed that the Prime Minister had seen Robertson and, as a result, had initiated activity amongst Australian officials in London. So far that event has not been authenticated.

Be that as it may, Lyons certainly interviewed Robertson, probably by telephone, soon after hearing from Crutchley. The Board chairman was told that the government viewed the situation most seriously, and more significantly that if the cricket crisis was not settled quickly the government feared that its attempts to negotiate a lower rate of interest on its London money market loans might well be jeopardised. Robertson agreed to do what he could and Hutcheon, chairman of the sub-committee, was asked to see Warner in Brisbane where the English team was waiting to see if the tour would proceed. Lyons telephoned Crutchley for confirmation of a possible change in field placings.

The negotiations were tough on both sides. Crutchley rang Warner to test the water about a field modification, and was told in no uncertain terms that for the MCC it was 'quite impossible to agree to any condition being attached to the withdrawal of the obnoxious word'. When the Australian Board sounded out its constituents, it found opposition from the players. Jeanes, for example, reported that Woodfull considered the Board had done nothing from which it need withdraw. Given both the Australian disarray and the English influence, the Board was never able to tough it out.

A particular strength on the English side was Ernest Crutchley's close personal friendship in Canberra with a key member of Australia's fledgling External Affairs branch, later the Department of Foreign Affairs. Frank Keith Officer was born in 1889, educated at Melbourne Grammar, graduated in law from the University of Melbourne, and went to the bar in 1914. He came from a prominent Tasmanian family. In the First World War he served at Gallipoli, like others in this drama, and won a Military Cross. He then joined the British Colonial Service to work in Nigeria. In the mid-1920s he returned to the new department in Canberra.

Officer had been in close contact with the cricket world throughout the bodyline crisis, as his diaries now held in the Australian National

Library reveal. He was in Melbourne for the Christmas period, as was Crutchley, and saw some of the test match there as well as speaking at length with the English team, especially Warner. Back in Canberra Officer and Crutchley dined together constantly throughout the Adelaide events and their immediate aftermath. Officer was thoroughly imbued with the idea of Empire and things British. The balance of his advice to Crutchley would have been to hold firm in the interests of the imperial spirit. His other invaluable service to Crutchley was in providing a close connection with establishment, Anglophile sections of society in Melbourne and Sydney. Officer thus helped Crutchley overcome some of the High Commissioner's social disabilities brought on by background and status. He also had very strong connections with Australian officialdom in London through contacts provided by his close friend R.G. Casey, later one of Australia's great political figures and Governor-General of Australia.

With this support, Crutchley was bound to win the concession he sought without the MCC having to yield any ground at all. According to a handwritten note in the Board's archives, Crutchley even offered a means by which the Australians might save some face—to 'sack Jeanes and make him the public scapegoat' for what happened in Adelaide. Presumably negotiations would then be started anew. Crutchley's great advantage was that through Officer and Casey he knew the government's anxiety because of the conversion loan issue, to maintain goodwill with the imperial power. The Board, on the other hand, had little knowledge about the impact of bodyline on wider politics.

The English team barely allowed the Board time to think. As if the telegram issue was not enough, co-manager Palairet threatened to cancel matches in Queensland because of an entertainment tax levied on gate-takings. Stand seats, for example, cost five shillings; the total tax was five pence of which the MCC share was proposed at one penny. Palairet argued that this was an unwarranted inroad into his team's tour profits. The Board was asked to adjudicate, giving it yet another difficult decision.

Plum Warner was responsible for opening both lines of political communication—the one in Adelaide which led to official notification of the affair in London, and that at the federal level, through Crutchley, which was also to reach imperial political authorities. Having done that, at the meeting with Hutcheon in Brisbane organised by Robertson at

Lyons's request, he declared himself a non-combatant. So far as he was concerned, bodyline was a matter for the official committees of the MCC and the Australian Board. It may be that he was now confident the MCC held the balance, or that he was worried by the exploding magnitude of the affair. He may have thought that his absence from the bargaining would ensure an MCC victory. Ills willings contain elements of all those possibilities. Like Robertson, the pressure was telling on Warner.

Meanwhile the ripples on the political pool widened. Lyons's main concern was with reaching a satisfactory position on the London conversion loans. On 24 January he spoke by telephone to his special minister for the negotiations in London, S.M. Bruce. They concluded, according to archival records, that they were faced with 'a most serious and fate-fraught decision'. Though that view applied to the loans issue specifically, the bodyline publicity cannot have caused them much peace of mind. Lyons thought they were involved not simply in economic bargaining, but also dealing with public opinion. He described it as a psychological attitude between Australians and the English, considering that the Australian public thought British authorities 'callous' in their treatment of Australian financial arrangements. If so, then the ill-feeling produced by bodyline must have added considerably to such a public attitude, something which would explain Lyons' mention of the conversion loans in his discussion with the Board chairman. His London emissary agreed with him, cabling on 9 February 1933: 'Greatest necessity is that during this critical period nothing should be done in Australia to imperil what is a most delicate situation.'

Given that Crutchley was privy to developments on the loans, bodyline must have been in mind during the composition of that cable. That is even more likely when it is remembered that many lengthy Canberra–London telephone calls occurred, at a cost of £2 per minute! It is now impossible to determine the precise content of those calls, or even to trace all the calls made. Given the supporting evidence, though, and the timing of the calls, it is highly probable that discussion occurred on bodyline and its possible solutions.

This informal level of activity is critical but undocumented, as in the case of cabinet discussion. Neither Australian nor British cabinet records reveal any formal discussion of bodyline. But, again, it is more

106

than likely the issue was discussed 'off the record', before or after meetings. Circumstantial evidence points to that in the British case, at least. Late in 1934, when memories of bodyline were still vivid, the secretary to the British cabinet, later Lord Hankey, visited Australia. He was an influential British interwar figure, like Gubby Allen with strong parental connections with Australia. During his tour he sent a report to the Dominions Office assessing the Australian situation. He reported that, deep down, Australians admired the British. To demonstrate that he drew an example from the 1932–33 tour of which he clearly had a detailed knowledge and a political viewpoint: 'It is because of this admiration that they felt so bitterly about the ridiculous bodyline bowling controversy. They hated to feel that we had lowered our standard of sportsmanship.' Given these strong views, it is most unlikely that no discussion of bodyline occurred in England. After all, many cabinet ministers were also MCC members, Stanley Baldwin for one. That view is strengthened further by the activities of Lyons's London representative. While Warner's Crutchley connection clearly influenced the official London view, Bruce managed to maintain the presence of an Australian view, an influence which helped considerably in the final resolution of the crisis.

Stanley Melbourne Bruce was born in Melbourne in 1883, into a family whose pastoral interests had helped create a major trading company. Educated at Melbourne Grammar, he went to Cambridge between 1904 and 1908. In 1908 he rowed in the winning eight, and later wrote a rowing manual. He was also a keen and reasonable cricketer. Bruce was admitted to the English bar in 1908. During the war he, too, served at Gallipoli, and on his return to Australia in 1918 was elected to federal parliament. In 1921–23 he was Treasurer, then won power in a coalition government and served as Prime Minister from 1923 until 1929 when he lost his seat. By 1931 he was back in parliament and by late 1932 was beginning a long stint in London, first as representative minister there then, from late 1933, as High Commissioner. Bruce loved things English, respected deeply the English way of doing things, and believed thoroughly in the principle of Empire.

During the first month of frantic bodyline politicking, Bruce was constantly meeting influential individuals in London. Much of this was because of the conversion loans but, being keenly attuned to public opinion generally, he would have been also involved in discussions of bodyline. On 12 January, for example, he lunched with Sir Samuel Hoare, at that point Secretary of State for India and highly placed in cabinet and on 17 January he spoke to the Royal Empire Society. Two days after the Board's first telegram he had a meeting with Sir Walter Elliott, Minister for Agriculture. On 25 January he was at the Dominions Office where undoubtedly bodyline figured in his discussions with senior officials. He lunched with Sir Philip Cunliffe-Lister, Secretary of State for the Colonies, on 2 February. It is highly probable that he saw Hore-Ruthven. He also met regularly and regarded highly Lord Hailsham, Leader of the House of Lords and about to become MCC President. In all, then, he was well placed to monitor and respond to whatever political initiatives were taken by the MCC in London.

In Australia, the Board found itself rapidly losing the battle. Between them, Crutchley and Warner worked on the crucial Queensland–New South Wales faction of the Board. While Crutchley lobbied the Sydney men, Warner and the touring team travelled to Brisbane for the test, which was still in jeopardy, in company with Hartigan and Hutcheon. Discussions begun on that journey were continued in Brisbane, with Warner keeping in close contact with Crutchley. Warner made it quite clear that the fourth test would not proceed unless the word 'unsportsmanlike' was withdrawn. What with that and the political pressure to which it was subjected, the Board soon had to withdraw its earlier statement. The MCC replied to the new telegram on 2 February, driving home its advantage: 'May we accept this as a clear indication that the good sportsmanship of our team is not in question?' The Board could scarcely reply, 'No'. Robertson sent out for approval a 'yes' response to the MCC, and by 8 February had the majority of agreements needed. The fourth test was out of danger.

There is an intriguing possibility that R.G. Menzies—then Attorney-General of Victoria, later Prime Minister and Sir Robert—was involved in drafting the second and third Australian cables. An Australian journalist of the time, Herbert Mishael, commented years later that rumours of Menzies's involvement were numerous in Melbourne. Menzies's interest in cricket was as great then as it was later, when political matters in England invariably coincided with test series and he was closely in touch with the Victorian Cricket Association. He would have had access to the Board members in Melbourne, and his advice probably would have been appreciated, especially when the cricket authorities were confronted with Prime Minister Lyons. Menzies might also have had a close knowledge of the English side—he had a close friendship with Plum Warner which lasted until Warner's death. It was Menzies who created the term 'Cathedral of Cricket' for Lord's which Warner became fond of using, and as Warner records in his *Cricket Between the Wars* the two men sat together through the Adelaide test. Unfortunately the Menzies papers now available contain no references to the period before 1935, so the possibility of his involvement awaits confirmation from other evidence.

In the course of just three weeks, then, the relatively simple fact of two Australian batsmen being struck by an English bowler had grown into a major imperial problem at the highest political levels. While those most directly involved, the cricketers, became almost secondary players the ramifications of bodyline became increasingly complex. It was inevitable that the Australian Board withdraw its unsportsmanlike label of Jardine's team, given the MCC advantages of cohesion and access to political influence. But that was a short term victory, and once the withdrawal was achieved what became interesting was the long term resolution of the conflict. In that, Australia was better placed as the Adelaide connection's access to Hore-Ruthven, and the Bruce presence in London combined into a reasonably effective lobby power. That was to show through in the London political reactions and, ultimately, in the aftermath of bodyline.

6
The aftermath

England won the fifth test in Sydney at the end of February 1933 to take the series by the convincing margin of four to one. After a tie with Victoria in Melbourne and a draw with South Australia in Adelaide, the MCC tour reached its final conclusion. When the MCC party left Sydney for New Zealand on 16 March, to undertake the previously disputed short tour, not a single member of the Australian team attended the reception which the New South Wales Cricket Association had organised at the Hotel Australia. As Jeanes had noted in a cable to Bushby, the Tasmanian delegate, there was an 'entire absence of good fellowship between the teams'.

This subdued departure was in stark contrast to the MCC's arrival in Sydney the previous November. On that occasion, again at the Hotel Australia, among those making welcoming speeches were the Premier of New South Wales, the Mayor and the Postmaster-General on behalf of the Prime Minister. The contrast could not have gone unnoticed, especially to the sensitive Empire loyalist Pelham Warner. Pataudi, Palairet and, most significantly, Harold Larwood did not travel with the party to New Zealand. The latter was en route to England nursing a badly damaged foot which he had sustained in the final test.

Financially the tour had been a huge success. If crowd attendances and gate receipts were the only criteria, then Lord's and the Australian Board would have been very satisfied. During the second test in Melbourne the attendance of 68 238 on the third day set a new world record for a cricket test. While the total match attendances at Adelaide and Brisbane are still (in 1983) the highest on record for those particular grounds.

Total attendance at the five tests numbered 761 163 which resulted in takings of £69 970. A reserved seat at Sydney or Adelaide cost 4s, whereas Melbourne was slightly cheaper at 3s 6d. Places in the outer, which often meant standing, cost 2s 1d in Sydney and 2s 4d in Adelaide. Test match admission prices were approximately double the rates for interstate matches. In 1933 the average male weekly wage in Australia was £3. Five or six days play, plus travel expenses, food and drink, for one or more likely two people, would account for a large proportion of the weekly wage packet. But unlike other matches during the depression, the crowds flocked in and very often were to be found queuing outside the grounds from the early hours of the morning.

The New South Wales Cricket Association, which hosted two tests, recorded a profit of £5052, its most successful season financially for the duration of the 1930s. The Victorian Cricket Association's net profit was smaller at £2746, but apart from the 1936–37 season, when two tests were played in Melbourne, this was another financial highpoint for the decade. The Australian Board must have been delighted as both the West Indies tour in 1930–31 and the South African visit during the 1931–32 season had lost money.

The MCC, under the tough treasureship of Dick Palairet, made a tour profit of £9571, a figure considerably in excess of their highest expectations. The profit gave the English counties renewed pecuniary vigour, as *Wisden* in 1933 stated: 'For the moment even the shakiest of counties must feel encouraged to battle on, seeing that they may reasonably expect a substantial sum of money as the result of the profits made by the MCC tour to Australia.' The cancellation of the remainder of the tour after the third test in Adelaide would have been a serious financial blow to the English counties. As well as lost income, the 1934 tour to England would also have been cancelled and with it would have disappeared lucrative funds. Taking both tours into account the English press estimated that each county would have lost £2000 if the MCC came home in mid-tour.

The popularity of the Australia-England test matches in 1932–33 and 1934 arose from a number of inter-related factors—the intense rivalry between the two countries as well as between the players themselves, improved public transport and technological innovations through radio coverage. Bodyline action on the field certainly drew the crowds but, equally, so did the batting skills of Donald Bradman. Whether Bradman was batting, or there was the likelihood of his appearance at the crease, made an appreciable difference to the attendance and,

Tom Glover's impression of Pelham Warner and Dick Palairet from
Owzat (1932)

consequently, gate receipts. It is not surprising that press adverts would announce that Bradman was to play. According to recent studies by Richard Cashman of Australian state games in the period 1930–40, there was an increase of 91 per cent amongst the crowd when the 'Don' was due to bat. Bradmania was rampant. Here was a batting genius from the bush with whom hundreds of thousands of working people could identify. Bradman was one of them who had made good.

The continual extension of transport facilities in Australia made access to the cities hosting the test matches easier and more comfortable. The NSW railways board had invested in considerable track extension programmes which were coming to fruition in the early 1930s as other existing lines were being electrified. For the first and fifth tests in the 1932–33 series, special excursion trains to Sydney ran on all lines in New South Wales. Furthermore, in an early attempt to market test cricket, the railways board and the NSW Cricket Association offered special rail and ground admission tickets. For 7s 6d the purchaser could obtain a five-day ticket for the fifth and final test—a 28 per cent saving. These reduced price tickets could only be bought at country railway stations in conjunction with rail tickets. A total of 297 packages were sold for the fifth test.

In 1932 the Sydney Harbour Bridge had been opened, which improved road traffic as well as giving the trams and railways greater access to the city's suburbs. The Bridge was another symbol and achievement which gave a depression-torn country hope for the future. By 1933 there was a government bus service in Sydney which complemented the extensive tram network, and this was also an era when the motor car grew in popularity, accessibility and influence. The price to the customer had been steadily falling and more consideration given to comfort for the driver and passengers. In 1921 only 2.1 per cent of the NSW population owned a motor vehicle but by 1933 the proportion had risen to 8.6 per cent. The overall effect of all these changes in transport policy was to make the great conurbations, like Sydney and Melbourne, within easy reach of the suburban or country population.

While tens of thousands flocked to see the bodyline series those that stayed at home, for the first time, could hear an up-to-the-minute commentary on the radio. The Australian Broadcasting Commission went to air on 1 July 1932 with an estimated potential audience of two million listeners. The 1932–33 tests were the first international cricket matches to be fully broadcast. Like cricket, radio was considered to have a significant role to play in the maintenance and consolidation of the imperial connection. On 26 December 1932 King George V made the first Christmas broadcast to Australia in which he commented: 'I take it as a good omen that wireless should have reached its present perfection at a time when the Empire has been linked in closer union, for it offers us immense possibilities to make the union still closer.'

Radio could certainly be used to unify the Empire but it also brought into people's homes controversial events like the third test in Adelaide. When Oldfield was hit on the head by Larwood the crack could be heard all round the ground and in the houses and gardens of all those listening, as could the roars of disapproval of the crowd. Ironically the bodyline broadcasts by the ABC were compromising the ties with the so-called mother-country, but the fault lay not with the radio, but with Jardine's and the MCC's tactics.

Cricket, being common to every state in Australia and because it highlighted the Empire connection, was an ideal candidate for extensive radio coverage. Ken Inglis, in *This is the ABC*, discusses these important connections:

> When the Commissioners wrote in their first Annual report of the characteristics of Australian society which broadcasts had to take into account, they mentioned in successive phrases 'the keen national interest in sport' and 'our position as part of the British empire and British race'.

Inglis considers that 'bodyline bowling enlarged the wireless audience' and due to the success of the coverage 'from that season on, test cricket had the right of way over other ABC programmes'.

The ABC endeavoured to maintain continuous reporting but when, on occasions as happened during the tests at Adelaide and Brisbane, there were no free landlines they constructed a commentary from telegram messages. A similar technique was used to cover the 1934 series in England. Called 'synthetic cricket' a telegram was despatched at the end of each over which contained the basic information about the play relating to the previous six balls. As the telegram arrived in Sydney it was phoned through to the ABC studios where a script was written for the two commentators to describe the game on a ball by ball basis.

The aftermath

For greater authenticity sound effects were added and past inter-nationals, like Monty Noble, added expert comments. This extensive coverage in Australia compares favourably and starkly with the two ten minute bulletins, plus an occasional thirty minute feature, which emanated from the BBC in London. The ABC's faith in cricket paid a handsome reward in the form of an unprecedented rate of growth in the purchase of radio licences.

Between the end of the tour in March and 28 April there was a hiatus in the stream of telegrams between London and the Australian Board in Adelaide. In the meantime the MCC Committee moved to deal with the problem of hot stories and inside information being leaked to the press as the tour party arrived home. The players had signed contracts which forbade them speaking to the press during the course of the tour but the concern felt at headquarters warranted a cable being despatched which warned the party about releasing 'information which was of a confidential nature'.

The most immediate danger was Harold Larwood. He was due to arrive on the *Otranto* on 2 April in Port Said. On 24 March Findlay sent a coded telegram to Larwood, which read: 'Feel certain you will regard matters connected with the tour strictly private and not give any information to friends including Mr Carr or Press who may meet you Port Said or elsewhere. Cable me Lords saying you will be on your guard.'

Arthur Carr was Larwood's captain at Nottinghamshire. He had captained England in the first four tests against Australia in 1926 in England and felt very bitter at the way he had been deposed from the captaincy to be replaced by the more socially acceptable and easy going Percy Chapman. Although an amateur Carr, like Jardine, was a captain who put winning above all else. Unlike Jardine he had a reputation for an overfondness for alcohol. Carr had encouraged Larwood and Voce to bowl bodyline for Nottinghamshire. That Carr was in Port Said at the behest of the *Daily Sketch* did not pass unnoticed at Lord's. The danger for the MCC was all too obvious—Larwood would speak to his club captain and the full story, or at least part of it, would be splashed across the country by Fleet Street. The Nottinghamshire Club Committee passed a resolution which criticised Carr's journey in the most forceful terms: 'strongly deprecated as being likely to damage Larwood's position with the MCC and to embarass the latter'.

115

When the MCC Committee met on 24 April Lord Belper was asked to reiterate to Larwood the importance of keeping silent. Belper was a former President of Nottinghamshire, a member of the Club Committee shortly to be elected to the MCC Committee—though in *Cricket with the Lid Off* Carr makes some disparaging comments on his knowledge of cricket. Also at this meeting, Jardine's request that he be allowed to write a number of articles about the bowling controversy and the tour came up for discussion. The Committee were adamant in refusing any such notion. They passed a resolution that they felt 'strongly that no publication by you or any member of the team should be made to the press before you have made your official report'.

For the Australian Board the central issue was the 1934 tour to England. Should it be cancelled? They decided that before they would commit themselves to sending a team they would want an assurance that bodyline bowling would not be used again. The Board's representative in England was Dr Robert 'Robbie' MacDonald who lived in Leicester and worked as a dentist. He had played for Queensland at the turn of the century and scored a half-century against the 1903 MCC team captained by Pelham Warner. In his eleven appearances for Queensland he gained a reputation as a slow, painstaking batsman. MacDonald also played for Leicestershire for whom he was honorary secretary in 1922-29. He had taken a keen interest in the controversial 1921 Australian tour and had spent a lot of time travelling around the country with the party.

MacDonald had already been involved in negotiations at Lord's in 1932 over the dispute about the forthcoming tour's finances and the MCC's desire to visit New Zealand. In May 1932 he was called to headquarters to discuss the matter with Lord Hawke, and the seriousness of these issues was indicated by the presence of David Maughan, a Kings Counsel, to help represent the Board. During the height of the bodyline crisis MacDonald had been out of the country but he returned to Leicester on 20 February 1933. He wasted no time and on 13 March he cabled the Board to inform them: 'Unmistakeable evidence growing feeling England against adoption body bowling respectfully submit we should maintain inflexible attitude making tour next year conditional on ban.'

At the Board meeting in Sydney on 30 January, a decision had been taken to establish a small sub-committee to examine the various options to eradicate the existence of bodyline bowling in Australia. The four members of the sub-committee were Roger Hartigan, a Queensland delegate to the Board, Bill Woodfull, the Australian captain, Victor Richardson, a well-respected and established Australian batsman and Monty Noble, one of Australia's greatest batsman who had captained Australia against England in 1903–04 when Pelham Warner led the MCC tourists.

The sub-committee proposed that a delivery bowled at the batsman 'with the intent to intimidate or injure him shall be considered unfair and "No-ball" shall be called'. Repeated offences could lead to the umpire debarring the bowler from participating any further during the course of that particular innings. On 28 April these recommendations were cabled to Lord's for the consideration of the MCC Committee.

The Board had to wait until 12 June for a reply. In the meantime there was much activity at Lord's in the wake of the tour. Harold Larwood finally arrived in Nottingham by train in early April. According to the *Observer* 20 000 people people turned out to greet him. Jardine and the rest of the players returned by ship from New Zealand, having drawn both tests there, and docked on 6 May in Glasgow to a tumultuous welcome. On the quay a pipe band played a serenade, while at the railway station, where they were due to catch a train south, a crowd of 10 000 waved them off. Jardine must have been thrilled by the landing in his native Scotland. By the time the train arrived in London only Jardine, Brown, Bowes, Ames and Tate were still aboard, but the reception was no less stirring. The conquering heroes had returned home.

Three days later Jardine, sporting a top hat instead of a harlequin cap, along with Dick Palairet, went to Lord's to begin their official report. Their reception at headquarters was no doubt rapturous. Feeling within the MCC was running high after the victories in the test matches and in what an Adelaide newspaper had called the 'cable rubber'. When the Annual General Meeting of the MCC gathered on 3 May the replies the Committee had sent were 'approved' amidst great applause. Later a celebratory tour dinner was announced for 19 July at the Dorchester hotel. The Prince of Wales had been invited but found himself unable to attend. Stanley Baldwin expressed his delight and duly accepted. The tickets cost 30s per head (more than half the amount of money most people earned in a week). The members were asked to wear a short coat, black tie and no military medals. The Committee decided that there would not be a band.

As was customary a new MCC President was announced at the Annual General Meeting. The outgoing President is not obliged to consult any other members of the Committee about who is to be his successor but given the events of the past few months it is certain that a small group on the Committee would have been privy to the decision. Lord Hawke's position as the most influential elder statesman would have ensured that he was fully consulted about the choice.

Viscount Lewisham nominated as his successor Viscount Hailsham, an intriguing political choice but also quite natural. He was a political heavyweight, at the time Secretary of State for War and a leading Conservative minister in MacDonald's National government. He had maintained an interest in cricket since his school days and in 1931 had assumed the presidency of the Sussex County Club. Befitting a person of his social standing, he had been a member of the MCC all his life, and was a member of the Carlton Club.

Viscount Hailsham had been born Douglas McGarel Hogg. He had been educated at Eton, but instead of going to university he went to work for the family firm of sugar growers in the West Indies. Like Sir Stanley Jackson he fought in South Africa during the Boer War and had a real 'Boy's Own' escape when a potentially fatal bullet was diverted by his silver flask! He was called to the bar in 1902 but following the death of his father chose to continue the latter's work with Kynaston Studd at the Regent Street Polytechnic in London. Like Jackson and Bridgeman he had been nominated to the Privy Council. In 1922 he won the parliamentary seat of St Marylebone for the Conservatives. Lord's stood in his constituency. He promptly joined the government as Attorney-General when Bridgeman was Home Secretary. When Baldwin took over as Prime Minister he retained Hailsham in his government. For two months, in 1928, he was acting Prime Minister.

Hogg was created Baron Hailsham in 1928, became a Viscount in 1929, and was Leader of the House of Lords and Secretary of State for War from 1931 onwards. As a leading figure in government he attended both the Ottawa Imperial Conference in 1932 and the World Economic Conference in 1933. His reputation as a diplomat markedly increased when he saved the cabinet from splitting over the trade issue. He proposed that collective cabinet responsibility be waived to allow both the free traders and the tariff protectionists to remain within the government. Contemporary historians have judged him as hard-working, but lacking in inspiration. Failing Baldwin, the MCC could not have appointed a more senior and experienced Tory politician to the presidency.

The MCC decided to establish a sub-committee to enquire into controversial events during the Australian tour. It comprised seven members: Hailsham, Hawke, Lewisham, Studd, Jackson, Lacey and Leveson-Gower. They were empowered to interview any members of the tour party with the goal of preparing a complete report for the full Committee by 12 June at the latest. Jardine and Palairet were the first to be called. The MCC Committee minutes show that only Bill Voce and Harold Larwood, from among the players, were interviewed. None of those who opposed bodyline bowling, such as the two amateurs Gubby Allen or the de facto vice-captain Bob Wyatt, were asked to appear. Warner was not in London when the sub-committee began to meet—he had stopped over in the United States on the return journey from New Zealand—but he did send a written report. Later he gave his views in person and according to Fingleton's book, *Cricket Crisis*, it was a dramatic performance: 'Newshawks who peered through the window were stirred to see Warner bobbing and ducking as if demonstrating the actions of an Australian batsman against bodyline.'

Given the choice of witnesses, the outcome of the sub-committee was a foregone conclusion. Their report does not appear to have survived but from the telegram sent by the MCC to the Australian Board on 12 June it is easy to ascertain its recommendations. To summarise that lengthy telegram, the Committee considered that 'the term "body-line" bowling is misleading and improper'; that the Australians were confusing 'body-line' with leg-theory; that it was 'improper and incorrect' to imply that an English bowler would deliver a 'direct attack' on the batsman; and that the new law the Australians proposed was not 'practicable'. The Committee having dealt with that contentious aspect of the controversy launched an offensive over the barracking of their team by the Australian spectators, which they considered at times 'thoroughly objectionable' and which the Board had failed 'to interfere, or to control'. Through their interpretation of events the Committee chose to ignore the circumstances which led to such heated feelings by the Australian spectators. Besides, by raising the hoary issue of

119

barracking the MCC Committee could divert some attention away from the bodyline question and appear less defensive.

From Findlay's correspondence it is clear that Jardine saw the 12 June telegram before it was despatched. In a letter to Stanley Christopherson, a member of the Committee, Findlay wrote: 'I am so glad you approve of the cable. I don't suppose Australia will. Jardine seems pleased at any rate.' He had every reason to be pleased! He had always harboured doubts about how much support he could count on from Lord's, but now they were standing firmly beside him, despite the fact that pressure was beginning to mount from those who had been in Australia and seen bodyline in action.

Jardine appeared firmly ensconced as England's captain. He was asked to lead the England team in the summer's three tests against the West Indies as well as being made captain of the Gentlemen's eleven to meet the Players. The leadership of the forthcoming tour to India during the English winter of 1933–34 appeared a foregone conclusion. The issue was decided at a special MCC Committee meeting on 10 July, which all the members, with the exception of Viscount Hailsham, attended. The matter was 'carefully considered' and 'after prolonged discussion' Jardine was offered the job. The meeting further decided that Hailsham and Hawke would talk with Jardine. The purpose and content of that small gathering are unknown but Jardine must have begun to feel that his previous unease about the Committee was becoming a reality.

Dr MacDonald's optimism was increasing as the English summer wore on. In the space of eight days he twice cabled Jeanes. On 21 June he endeavoured to reassure the Board that an 'overwhelming majority English players support Australian opinion bodyline bowling'. Just prior to the end of month he urged them to 'hold up any reply to Marylebone had important interview Sir Stanley Jackson at Lords'.

Through a more considered letter to Jeanes, dated 11 July, MacDonald was able to outline the contents of his 'long chat' with Jacker. The gist of the matter was that 'He seemed to be most sympathetic to our Australian view regarding bodyline bowling, and went so far as to assure me that "it was not likely to be used against us again".' Jackson later reassured MacDonald that he would 'see the other members of the MCC sub-committee', and proposed a further meeting. MacDonald was ecstatic: 'His influence at MCC is of course a

very great one, and I was left *in no doubt* from our long conversation
that he is *strongly opposed* to the type of bowling Jardine used against
us.'

Jackson had always considered that he would have been capable of
playing bodyline bowling, although it should not be forgotten that he
never toured Australia and thus did not play on very fast wickets. John
Marshall, in his book, *Lord's*, recalls visiting Jackson: 'Standing in the
study of his London home in Pont Street he demonstrated to me just
how he would have dealt with fast, rising balls coming in his direction.
With a malacca cane he hooked them right off his neat cavalry
moustache.' Jackson's previously stated views on bodyline had varied
between ambiguity and confusion but now it appeared he had reached a
definite decision to oppose it. At the height of the crisis, just after the
meeting at the Dominions Office with Jimmy Thomas on 1 February,
Jackson was quoted in the *News Chronicle*: 'The tests must continue at
all costs, cancellation is too absurd. We can solve the troubles all right.
We must not assume that all wrongs are on one side and all rights on the
other. We must see each other's point of view and must give and take.'
In February the lines had been so firmly drawn that there was no room
for compromise or conciliation. As time passed and a real picture of the
events that had transpired in Australia became more apparent, Jackson
pressed for appeasement but on the MCC's terms.

A critical turning point in the English discussion about bodyline
came on 22 July when the second test against the West Indian tourists
began at Old Trafford. The West Indies fast bowlers, Learie Constantine and Manny Martindale, bowled bodyline against England. The
West Indian team were very keen to win one test during their second
tour of England. Such a victory would be an important influence in
gaining recognition for West Indian cricket. Furthermore, attendances
on the tour had not been good and press comment rather unfavourable.
Employing bodyline bowling tactics and exploiting their fast bowlers to
the full might solve all the problems. But Old Trafford was not a fast
Australian wicket and Constantine and Martindale lacked the extra
speed and accuracy of Harold Larwood. During the second England
innings Jardine scored his first century in test cricket, which further
increased his personal stature in the public mind. He had shown that
bodyline could be played and the Australians really were just squealers.

Altham and Swanton describe the consequences of the second test in

A History of Cricket: 'No accurate comparison could be made with Australia, it did cause a considerable body of knowledgable cricketers and critics to shift their opinion on fast leg-theory bowling, whether from ethical or aesthetic considerations or both.' No doubt Altham included himself as one much knowledgable critic who changed his mind. When the crisis broke in January 1933 he had written in the *Observer* that the Australians had been 'frightened out' and that an 'ignorant public opinion' was being 'exploited by an hysterical press'.

The Australian proposal for changes in the laws of the game to eradicate bodyline bowling was on the agenda of the Imperial Cricket Conference scheduled to meet at 3.00 p.m. on 31 July. The ICC formally provided a link between the mother-country, in the shape of the MCC, and the dominions. As in diplomatic and foreign policy matters, all power remained with Britain and in the case of cricket, with the Marylebone Club. The composition of the ICC reflected the dominant position of the MCC. Viscount Hailsham took the chair and along with Lord Hawke represented the MCC. The Australians had two representatives, MacDonald and Mallett, who was also a member of the MCC Committee. In the circumstances it is understandable that Mallett expressed his concern at having a foot in two camps and that he might be forced to cease representing Australia. Plum Warner was one of South Africa's two delegates. India, in the person of General Sir C.H. Harington the Governor of Gibralter, New Zealand and the West Indies had one member each. Hailsham was confident in his ability to ensure a prompt conclusion to the meeting, which was to be followed at 4.30 by an MCC Committee meeting.

It seemed certain that the ICC delegates would reject the Australian proposal but, with the help of Jackson, MacDonald arranged for the item to be deferred to a future meeting when he hoped the situation would be more favourable. Of greater significance on 31 July were a series of informal meetings between MacDonald and leading members of the MCC. Earlier in the day he had spoken with Viscount Hailsham but at 6.00 p.m, after the MCC Committee had completed its business, he met with the real powers at Lord's—Hawke, Lewisham, Jackson and Findlay.

MacDonald, on behalf of the Australian Board, wanted an unequivocal assurance that bodyline would not be used against them on the 1934 tour. Unless they were given such a guarantee they would not send the tour party. From informal sources MacDonald knew that he could almost certainly extract such a promise. To begin with the MCC quartet were reluctant to commit themselves and suggested that they required more time to consider the matter. According to MacDonald's letters he responded that perhaps Australia might choose four fast bowlers. Hawke was aghast: 'Reprisals by God'. 'No I would call it reciprocity, merely mutual action and reaction', replied MacDonald. Point taken. It was agreed that Australia had the right to know if bodyline was a possibility, and MacDonald now received the assurance he had been seeking.

The MCC recognised that bodyline was not acceptable during the 1934 season in England but how could they continue to justify the public stand they had taken in January and February in backing Jardine? This was a dilemma that they were quick to note and they began to feel that the problem had arisen because they had backed Jardine 'prematurely'. They needed to extricate themselves from the situation without publicly losing face, while at the same time not be seen to be letting down the successful and popular Jardine. They had no intention of making any public statement that would recognise that the Australians had been correct or that either they or Jardine were at all culpable. With their own personal and political backgrounds, and in the context of strain between England and Australia, they adamantly refused to be seen to bow before a Dominion.

Part of the MCC cover-up rested on the word bodyline. They refused to recognise its existence. MacDonald told Jeanes that 'they take great exception' to its use. In the interests of diplomatic expediency MacDonald suggested that the Australians should use another more acceptable phrase 'that type of bowling in Australia to which exception was taken by Australia' instead of bodyline. This wonderful elliptical formulation was worthy of the best in British diplomacy.

The Dominions Office maintained a close interest in the bodyline crisis from March to June. The index to their file records the receipt of two letters from Ernest Crutchley which had been sent to Sir H Batterbee, a senior official. Sir Philip Game, the Governor of New South Wales, also sent a letter with his comments on the affair. But the most interesting entry is the record of a communication from Hore-Ruthven to Jimmy Thomas. The index lists the contents as 'comments upon the result of the cricket incidents and suggests a way of removing any misunderstandings between the two countries'. It was received in London on 21 June 1933 and must have been despatched from Adelaide shortly after Hore-Ruthven's return to Australia. Unfortunately, all these letters have been destroyed.

On another front, Australia made an important breakthrough which relieved potential pressure on the Board. On 17 July 1933 the British Chancellor of the Exchequer finally conceded as an 'exceptional measure' to permit the conversion of Australian loans on the London market to a lower and more reasonable rate. The tardiness of the British Treasury in accepting the conversion left a bitter taste with many Australian politicians. Scullin, a former Labor Prime Minister, commented: 'Sympathetic support by the treasury, banks and financial groups would have ensured the success of a large Australian conversion loan many months ago.' The Australian Board now felt in a good position from which to make a reply to the MCC cable of 12 June. This they did on 22 September. The two most significant paragraphs read:

> We note that you consider that a form of bowling which amounted to a direct attack by the bowler on the batsman would be against the spirit of the game. We agree with you that leg-theory bowling as it has been generally practised for many years is not open to objection. On these matters there does not appear to be any real difference between our respective views . . . We feel that while the type of bowling to which exception was taken in Australia strictly was not in conflict with the Laws of Cricket yet its continued practice would not be in the best interests of the game. May we assume that you concur in this point of view and that the teams may thus take the field in 1934 with that knowledge?

The word bodyline had disappeared.

When the MCC replied on 9 October they stated that not only did they welcome 'the friendly tone' but they presumed that any difference was 'on the question of fact'. They proceeded: 'Your team can certainly take the field with the knowledge and with the full assurance that cricket will be played here in the same spirit as in the past and with the single desire to promote the best interests of the game in both countries.' According to MacDonald, this was the public signal to Australia that bodyline would not be used during the forthcoming tour. Given the composition and style of the MCC Committee, the Board were led to understand that Lord's had entered into a gentlemen's agreement. 'The type of bowling in Australia to which exception was taken by Australia' found itself implicitly castigated as 'not cricket'.

MacDonald considered that this represented 'a complete victory for our Board' and a 'full vindication of Australia's objection to Jardine's methods', though to the public at large that was far from clear. There was no hint from Lord's that they condemned Jardine's tactics during the 1932–33 tour. Hailsham and the MCC Committee must have been pleased that the crisis had been diplomatically defused and that the threatened 1934 tour could proceed. Not all the delegates on the Australian Board saw the matter in that light.

The power centre of the Board had now shifted from Victoria to New South Wales with the election of Aubrey Oxlade, the Sydney solicitor, as the new chairman. Allen Robertson, having been chairman for the previous three years, was not eligible for re-election. Through this piece of good fortune Oxlade, who along with his fellow state delegates had urged caution from the outset when the controversy began in January, assumed leadership. During the Australian winter he won a majority for conciliation and appeasement. However a minority group of five Board members still pressed for a tougher stance. Robertson, with the support of the other Victorian delegates Mailer and Kelly as well as Hartigan and Hutcheon from Queensland, despatched a letter to the other members of the Board. They stressed that the 'time of conciliation has passed' and specifically that an 'assurance should be demanded'.

Fearful that his weeks of patient bridge-building and negotiating would be jeopardised, MacDonald cabled Adelaide on 21 October to reaffirm:

> Respectfully hope matter be regarded as gentlemens agreement.
> Marylebone position difficult . . . Risk of repetition bodyline
> infinitesimal. Overwhelming majority English captains and
> cricketers and all imperial conference delegates condemn it. Any
> attempt to reopen negotiations will be grave tactical mistake.
> Marylebone's cable promised warm welcome and every effort to
> make visit enjoyable. This assurance reveals the certain
> abandonment of bodyline.

The minority made no progress. Oddly, Hartigan and Hutcheon were in the conciliatory minority in January and now in a minority for tough

Farewell to bodyline

A cartoon from the Australian Cricketer, October 1933

action. The NSW Association, whose Executive Oxlade chaired, were delighted with the 'settlement' and even went so far as to express their 'entire accord with the wording of the recent cablegrams which passed between the two bodies.' At the same meeting they noted with pleasure that Bull, another of the NSW delegates to the Board, had been chosen to be treasurer on the 1934 tour to England, alongside Bushby, the Tasmanian delegate, who would be manager. In the New Year Honours' list Oxlade received the CBE 'for services to cricket', but actually for his part in resolving the issue.

Between 16 November and 14 December 1933 four more cables were exchanged between Adelaide and London but these contained little more than confirmations and mutual self-congratulation. During November the MCC Committee, having successfully accomplished its volte-face, passed a resolution which stated 'that any form of bowling which is obviously a direct attack by the bowler upon the batsman would be an offence against the spirit of the game'. On 23 November they presented this resolution to a joint meeting of the Board of Control of Test Matches at Home, and the Advisory County Cricket Committee. The latter comprised all seventeen county captains. The resolution was endorsed and it was understood that the captains would not countenance such 'direct attack' bowling in the English game. 'Direct attack' was an MCC euphemism for 'bodyline'.

Jardine, the Surrey captain, was unable to present his views at the 23 November meeting. The MCC tour to India, which he captained, had begun in mid-October and was to last until March 1934. The three-match test series was comfortably won by England two to nil with one drawn game in which Jardine's men dominated. Throughout this long tour, England lost only one match and that by the narrowest of margins. Jardine with 52.18 topped the batting averages but, more importantly, further established himself as one of England's most successful captains. Since 1931 under his leadership England had suffered only one defeat — the second test against Australia, in Melbourne, during the 1932–33 series.

Now the dispute with the Australian Board had been resolved amicably various members of the MCC Committee turned their attention to the thorny issue of Jardine's future when he returned from India. Plum Warner wrote to Hore-Ruthven on 3 January 1934:

The real trouble is Jardine. Is he to be Capt? At present I say 'No' unless he makes a most generous public gesture of friendliness and then I am not sure I would trust him. He is a queer fellow. When he sees a cricket ground with an Australian on it he goes mad! He rose to his present position on my shoulders, and of his attitude to me I do not care to speak. It is hoped he may retire at the end of the Indian tour, but in many quarters here—where they do not know the truth—he is a bit of a hero.

It would be safe to assume that Hore-Ruthven shared Warner's views, though more light on his opinions will be shed if a collection of his letters presently under permanent embargo are released from Lord's.

Warner reiterated the same views in a letter to Findlay on 22 February 1934. The knives were out:

Of course if Jardine were captain it might be awkward, but your conversation the other day led me to understand that Jardine would be required by MCC to give certain guarantees which would appreciably ease the situation. I believe you realise that I was his best friend and supporter. I have no axe to grind and my objections to his methods and manners was because I considered them contrary to the ideals and interests and the prestige of MCC . . .

I believe that history will find me guiltless of a wrong appreciation of the situation.

I do not consider that Jardine—on his Australian form—can produce the friendly relations and happy spirit which MCC so urgently desire in the coming test matches and which are so vital for the good of the game.

Warner had decided to put the game before all personal considerations. Jardine must go. Perhaps such behind-the-scenes manouevres were a habit! In 1926 he had lauded Arthur Carr and urged him to take the England captaincy, but within the space of a year had been instrumental in replacing him.

MacDonald was also endeavouring to exert pressure on Lord's for Jardine to be deposed. He sarcastically described Jardine's methods as 'wholly teutonic' and the man himself as comparable to 'Attila' and continued, in a letter to Jeanes, by stressing that he had urged Findlay that Jardine should be encouraged 'to devote himself *exclusively* to civic and personal matters'.

Both Warner and MacDonald, for the sake of the prestige and public status of the MCC, wanted Jardine to resign and go quietly. This would avoid an unfortunate public scene in which Jardine would be seen to be sacked and, most likely, gain further public support. Given his record as a test batsman and captain his removal would be impossible for the MCC to justify on grounds of ability.

Jardine did resign, but on his terms. On 31 March 1934 the *Evening Standard* printed an exclusive telegram from him in India. In no uncertain terms he stated that 'I have neither the intention nor the desire to play cricket against Australia this summer'. A few days later the same paper announced that Jardine would be covering the forthcoming series against Australia on their behalf.

The opportunity that Warner had been seeking now presented itself. He decided to raise the matter with the MCC Committee. On 1 May he wrote to Findlay:

> I venture to ask the Committee whether they intend to take any notice of Mr Jardine's cable to the *Evening Standard* of March 31, a copy of which I enclose.
>
> I desire to speak with restraint in this matter, but it seems to me that in Jardine's cable, which he knew was for public consumption, is in direct contradiction of MCC's called promises to Australia.
>
> The words 'no desire to play against Australia this summer' are really most discourteous and deliberately flout MCC's expressed wishes and desires; and Mr Jardine is a member of the cricket and selections committee of MCC. I beg to urge that the Committee consider this cable of Mr Jardine and whether any steps are necessary in connection with it.

Jardine had publicly flouted the MCC, but he must have known the way events at Lord's had been moving and that there was no possibility of his being able to use bodyline tactics against Australia in 1934. On paper his record as England captain was outstanding and at 33 perhaps he felt this was the time to retire. Besides he was shortly to be married and had a career in the city to pursue. To the end he did things his way.

The new selection committee nominated by the MCC was Sir Stanley Jackson, Tommy Higson and Percy Perrin. The latter two were connected to Lancashire and Essex respectively. Warner had been a member of the selection committee in 1931 and 1932 but in 1933 he was replaced by Lord Hawke and in 1934 there was still no place for him. He would have to wait until 1935 before he regained his membership of that committee. As a consequence of the bodyline controversy the *Australian Cricketer* also contended that he lost his knighthood. They wrote on 10 June 1933:

> It was fully expected that this year's list of birthday honours would
> have included a cricket knighthood. Mr Pelham Warner was
> expected to be the fortunate recipient of the honour to
> cricket . . . Owing to the cloud over the cricket atmosphere
> obviously a cricket honour would not have been in order.

Warner received a knighthood in 1937.

The 1934 selection committee chose Bob Wyatt, the Warwickshire amateur, as captain, although he proved to be unfit for the first test at Trent Bridge, Nottingham, and the honour passed to Cyril Walters, the Worcestershire captain and club secretary. Wyatt returned for the remaining four tests in a series in which Australia quickly regained the Ashes by a margin of two to one with two draws.

Despite the fact that the first test in 1934 was to be played on Larwood's home ground at Trent Bridge he was not selected. He followed in Jardine's footsteps by writing an article in the *Sunday Dispatch* on 17 June, on the eve of the team being announced for the second test, in which he categorically affirmed: 'I have definitely made up my mind not to play against the Australians in this or any of the tests.' His test career was now finished. A man with a reputation for speaking his mind, he saw no point in holding back. In the English county game he continued to take wickets and in 1936 topped the bowling averages. However, even if his own comments had not already done so, there was not the remotest possibility that he would be chosen for the 1936–37 tour to Australia under the captaincy of the Australian-born, non-bodyline bowling Gubby Allen. Bill Voce, who showed a more repentant attitude, did make that tour.

During the 1934 season Larwood and Voce bowled together for Nottinghamshire under the captaincy of Arthur Carr. After a stormy match against Lancashire at Trent Bridge a complaint was made to Lord's by Tommy Higson about the 'direct attack' bowling of the Notts pair. Higson was the Lancashire chairman, but more significantly a member of the test selection committee. He had been one of the selectors that chose Larwood and Voce to tour Australia in 1932–33 and was to remain on the selection committee until the end of the 1937 season. He had endorsed the first MCC cable, which threatened to cancel the tour, and made a speech at the Lancashire Annual General Meeting backing the MCC team in Australia, but his conversion to a position of opposing bodyline struck MacDonald with such force that he wrote on 2 January 1934 to Jeanes that Higson was 'a very warm friend of Australia. He adopted a very strong attitude during the past six months in supporting Australian contentions relating to the body-line controversy.' MacDonald even suggested that if Mallett persisted in his view that he was unable to represent Australia on the ICC, perhaps Higson would be a suitable replacement. In the end Mallett did not relinquish the responsibility.

Lancashire were not alone in complaining about the Notts bowlers. Middlesex voiced similar objections and particularly against Bill Voce. The Middlesex Committee met on 4 October and passed a resolution to 'register an emphatic protest against the manner in which Voce bowled'. Their feelings were conveyed in a letter signed by A.J. Webbe, the Middlesex President, member of the MCC Committee and an old friend of Warner, to the Notts chairman. The Committee at Trent Bridge felt obliged to apologise.

However the most significant incident involving bodyline bowling during the 1934 season occurred when the Australian tourists met Nottinghamshire on 11, 13 and 14 August. Neither Larwood nor Bradman played. Carr was another notable absentee. The Australian batsmen included Woodfull, Brown, McCabe, Kippax and Darling and for the first and only time on the tour, they were subjected to a barrage of bodyline bowling. Bill Voce took eight wickets in the Australian's first innings in a match which *Wisden* politely described as 'rendered unpleasant by the antagonistic attitude of the spectators towards the visitors'—in other words there was some barracking.

At the end of the second day when the Australians batted, Voce bowled a further two overs. During the night he contracted 'sore shins' and was unable to participate on the final day. The real and obvious reason for his non-appearance related to his contravention of the new-found spirit which condemned 'direct attack' bowling. Further, Bushby and Bull, the Australian manager and treasurer, had lodged a complaint against the 'intimidatory' bowling by Voce to the Notts Committee and the MCC. The Notts Committee apologised and expressed their deep regret to the tourists.

Arthur Carr rushed to Voce's defence both in private and in the press. As a direct consequence he was relieved of the captaincy to find himself another casualty of the cricket establishment's anti-bodyline crusade. Feeling was running high amongst the Notts members who, for the most part, supported Carr, Larwood and Voce. At the club's Annual General Meeting 2500 people turned up, and the Committee *en bloc* were forced to resign. As Carr rose to address the meeting the assembled crowd broke into song with 'For he's a jolly good fellow'.

This meeting, and the ovation that Jardine received when he played in Yorkshire for Surrey, indicate that strong public support still existed for bodyline and its exponents. Carr expressed a commonly held view in *Cricket with the Lid Off*: 'If Jardine's team won the Ashes fairly and squarely by certain methods in Australia (and the MCC maintained that the methods were fair and square) why were we not allowed to try and keep the Ashes by similar methods in this country?' Apart from the obvious point that there would have been no tour if such methods had been threatened, Carr's comment reinforces the view that it was not clear that the MCC now condemned those methods and did not think they were fair.

Jardine showed no signs of repentance. He considered that the exclusion of Voce from the England side to play in the final test at the Oval, especially after his success for Notts against the Australians, was 'quite inexplicable'. In Jardine's opinion this was yet another mistake made by a selection committee who were out of touch with the modern game and instead prefered a policy of appeasement. Jackson and Higson were the main culprits. In *Ashes and Dust* Jardine comments acidly that these two selectors had 'from the safe distance of some thousands of miles, categorically announced their disagreement with leg theory'. He continued by making a telling point that Jackson had failed to make any public criticism of the bodyline bowling methods of his fellow Yorkshireman, Bill Bowes.

A special meeting of the MCC Committee was called for 20 September 1934 as a consequence of Voce's bowling against the Australians and the complaint made to Lord's. Warner advocated a more forceful and stringent application of Law 43 that the 'umpires are the sole judges of fair or unfair play'. He pressed for the MCC to 'instruct umpires to act more frequently'. Bob Wyatt, the England captain, proposed the frequently suggested idea of a line across the wicket. The bowlers would be obliged to pitch the ball in the portion nearer to the batsman. This notion was firmly rejected by the Committee on 15 October with Sir Stanley Jackson expressing the strongest objections.

A week prior to this meeting the MCC had decided to establish another special sub-committee charged with 'eliminating this type of bowling from the game'. Among the sub-committee's members were Lord Hawke, Viscount Lewisham, Sir Stanley Jackson and Sir Kynaston Studd—four of the central figures within the MCC who had been involved in the bodyline crisis from the outset. It also included the new President, the second Earl of Cromer, Lord Hampden, Plum Warner and four respected and slightly younger former amateur players—Messrs Falcon, G.R. Jackson, Mallett and Twining. Their report was to be presented by 12 November 1934.

After the annual meeting of the Board of Control of Test Matches at Home and the Advisory County Cricket Committee, the MCC Committee issued a statement on 21 November which further clarified their position. They noted that during the previous season 'direct attack' bowling had occurred and that it 'may continue to develop if left unchecked'. On the recommendation of their sub-committee the MCC defined in more detail what they felt constituted a 'direct attack'. This was 'persistent and systematic bowling of fast short-pitched balls at the batsman standing clear of the wickets'. In line with Warner's previous suggestion, the umpires were urged to implement Law 43 against this practice. The county captains and their committees publicly resolved to take 'the strongest possible steps' to eliminate this type of bowling from the game.

Exactly two years after the England team had first used bodyline bowling against an Australian eleven at Melbourne, the MCC made their final and definitive statement against what they euphemistically called 'direct attack', and what to the rest of world was bodyline.

Conclusion

The *dramatis personae* of the bodyline controversy later went their own ways. After his retirement Douglas Jardine wrote a manual entitled *Cricket* and some newspaper articles on the subject, but retained only the loosest affiliation with the game and its administration. In 1934 he married Irene Peat, the daughter of Sir Harry Peat, senior partner in the Peat Marwick international accountancy firm which later became connected with the Price Waterhouse empire. Jardine pursued his intellectual interests, in religion for example, and tended business interests in landholding throughout the Empire—he was chairman of the New South Wales Land Agency Company, and on the board of the Scottish Australian Company, among others. During the Second World War he served in France, Belgium and India with the Royal Berkshire Regiment before returning to civilian life. Just before his death in 1958 he returned briefly to cricket, as president of the Oxford University Cricket Club between 1955 and 1957.

His daughter, Fiannach Lawry, remembers him as a man of discipline and duty who set himself, and others, standards which were much too high. The family version of the bodyline story is that Jardine was sent to Australia with instructions to employ bodyline tactics, and then let down during the post-tour negotiations. Though the material available does not support that view directly, circumstantial evidence does make it a possibility. Whatever else, Jardine certainly saw the matter through to the end, another trait remembered by his family. His single-mindedness and his strong beliefs in loyalty—imbibed from his father—showed through in the way he stopped attending church. When Edward the Eighth was forced to abdicate for constitutional reasons located in religion, Jardine became convinced he could no longer support such an institution. He turned increasingly to fishing and Eastern mysticism.

Conclusion

Harold Larwood never played test cricket again. His foot injury suffered during the bitter 1932–33 days cut him down to a medium pace bowler, and his post-tour remarks and attitude doomed him. He finished with 78 test wickets at an average of 28.41, one of those players of whom a brief exploit rather than a career is remembered. But, as Ian Peebles wrote, 'No contemporary cricketer believes that there was ever a faster bowler than Harold Larwood'. He lingered in county cricket until 1938, still enjoying success as in 1936 when he topped the bowling averages, and at his retirement had taken 1427 first class wickets at 17.51. After the Second World War he settled in Australia to live out a quiet life, apart from being questioned during periods of renewed interest in bodyline.

Sir Pelham Warner, as he became in Lord's sesquicentenary year of 1937, lived until 1963. He continued writing, including three major books: *Cricket Between the Wars* (in which bodyline features little), *Lord's* (a homage to the ground and to the MCC), and *Long Innings* his autobiography, (commemorating an unswerving devotion to a basically simple game). For a man so steeped in cricket traditions, it was perhaps appropriate that he died on the eve of England's first one-day competition, the Gillette Cup. It would have been no less perplexing for him than bodyline had been 30 years earlier. He probably never recovered fully from the psychological scars of 1932–33, which marred his otherwise unquestionable contribution to cricket development. The knighthood, the presidency of MCC in 1950 after long service, the naming of the Warner Stand at Lord's in 1958, and the 1961 first vice-presidency given for life in Lord's history must all have been great moments.

Views on Warner's contribution to the controversy must now be more mixed than earlier. The theme was once that he was an idealistic man who could not cope when pitched into a clash of wills with the indomitable Jardine, and there is certainly much evidence to support this. In the course of researching this book, however, an alternative view has emerged—that of a man willing to enlist political support to assist his case, and to vary his support from one side to the other as the moment dictated. Warner claimed to have been Jardine's greatest friend on the tour, but was quick to deny him back in England. The 'Cathedral of Cricket' (as he called Lord's) and its apostolic functions ranked first in his hierarchy of loyalties.

Sir Alexander Hore-Ruthven, who provided a major avenue for

official political manoeuvres on bodyline, remained in Australia until 1944. When his term as Governor of South Australia expired he was transferred to New South Wales, becoming Lord Gowrie, first Baron of Canberra and Dirleton, in 1935. In 1936 he became Governor-General of Australia, a post he held until 1944 because of the Second World War. In 1941 he was elevated to an earldom. Gowrie died in 1955, but he and his wife are still remembered in Australia through the Gowrie scholarship scheme (for the descendants of war service personnel) and the Lady Gowrie pre-school centres in cities and towns. It was Gowrie's work on bodyline which perhaps brought him the presidency of the MCC in 1948 not long after his return from Australia.

Ernest Crutchley, His Majesty's Government Representative in Australia during the crisis, returned to England in 1935 to become later an Assistant Under-Secretary of State in the Dominions Office. The post he left was upgraded to high commissioner status, a change which he had urged but did not come to enjoy himself. Crutchley died in 1940. His stay in Australia was never entirely comfortable, and his confidence in things British was tested by the bodyline tactics which he hated. He did everything he could to help his friend Warner and MCC win the battle, but made it very clear what he thought of their methods. Had that been known at the time, at least some Australian antipathy might have been placated.

On the Australian side, Don Bradman went from being a great player to one of the game's greatest. He became captain of Australia in 1936 and retained the post until his retirement at the end of the 1948 tour of England. By that point his test batting average stood at 99.94 runs per innings, a staggering achievement over a twenty-year period. His total of 29 test centuries came in only 80 innings, and was in no danger until Sunil Gavaskar surpassed it in 1983 after a far greater number of innings. At the end of his playing career Sir Donald (as he became in 1949) moved into cricket administration where he was as influential as on the field. A member of the Australian Cricket Board of Control for many years, he was chairman between 1960 and 1963, then again from 1969 to 1972. He was also president of the South Australian Cricket Association from 1965 until 1973. His stockbroking business flourished, and he became a director of many companies. In his spare time he was a good squash and billiards player, and a very fine golfer.

Bradman did not fail during the crisis but he was contained to 56.6

runs per innings, a modest effort for him and the difference between the sides. The pressure on him was enormous, not just to play well but also to cope with his health and his relations with the Board (the two were not unrelated). His love hate relationship with administrators, players and public alike was beginning to blossom. It could not have been easy to tolerate the jibes that his dancing tactics against the Larwood bouncers were born of fear. For those reasons, it is not surprising that Bradman was so reticent about the bodyline attack designed to curb his genius.

William Woodfull, Bradman's stoic captain, took the Australian side to England in 1934, then retired. Like Jardine he wrote a cricket manual but never an autobiography. For the most part, the minister's son devoted himself to schoolteaching in which career he became principal of Melbourne High School from 1956 until 1962. His pupils, like his cricketing colleagues, recall him as quiet and likeable, with a sense of proper form and responsibility. He died in 1965 having earned an Order of the British Empire and never having revealed publicly his version of the 1932–33 story. It is now clear, however, that he informed the Board at the time of his dislike for the tactics, dismay at their imperial implications and, probably, dissatisfaction with the Board's attempts to solve the problem. Whatever else, he held his players in line when feelings were running high, and that was no mean feat.

For cricketers, one of the major consequences of bodyline was a liberation of the fast bowler. While it is true that fast bowlers had always been menacing, during the years leading up to the crisis, the improvement of pitches in both England and Australia had generally moved the odds out of their favour. That, combined with an unwritten rule to keep the ball up, meant that by the 1920s batsmen were well favoured. The reputations of Spofforth, Jack Gregory, Ted McDonald and the like were generally gained either on poor wickets or under specific circumstances. Because their performances *were* out of the ordinary, they became the subject of great attention. That is not to detract from their memories; it is simply to indicate that their tasks became increasingly difficult.

Immediately after the 1932–33 season, fielding restrictions and a desire for tranquillity gave a breathing space for batsmen. The signs for the future were there, though, when the 1933 West Indians bowled short at Old Trafford, Manny Martindale taking 5 for 73 while Jardine

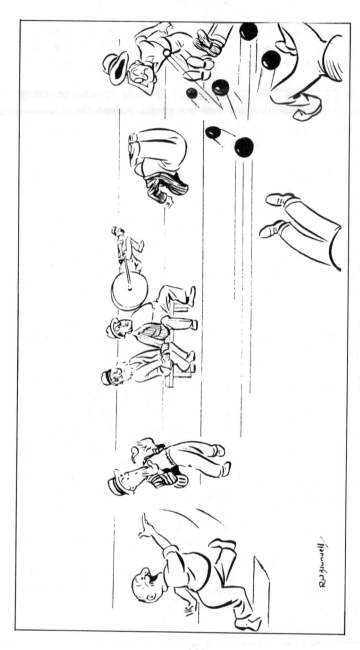

A former bodyliner plays bowls

R. W. Blundell's view of the future from Bodywhine (1933)

scored his only test century. After 1945 the restraints on fast bowlers were cast aside as the 'bouncer' or 'bumper' became a legitimate part of the repertoire. Lindwall and Miller for Australia, and Tyson and Trueman for England, matched each other through the 1950s, while the 1960s saw the rise of aggressive fast bowlers throughout the cricketing world. By the 1970s Lillee and Thomson were the scourge of England, and the West Indies were producing a string of such players: Roberts, Holding, Garner and Croft to name but four. However, in the 1970s and 1980s the response was batting helmets, not rule changes. Batsmen were no longer sacrosanct.

In a sense international cricket reached a watershed in 1932–33. There had long been fears that test cricket was too serious with too much national pride and aspiration attached. Bodyline marked a turning point in the business of serious cricket. There were 'friendly' tours after that, certainly—Gubby Allen and Freddy Brown, for example, led such sides in 1936–37 and 1950–51—but they were exceptions rather than the rule. Wally Hammond led the 1946–47 MCC team in Australia, and its controversies somehow set the pattern for much of what was to occur in succeeding years. The bodyline experience might have been solved in the short term, but its long-term impact is still with us in many ways.

Aubrey Oxlade's CBE possibly helped placate Australian cricket authorities in the wake of the Jardine tour, but the Board could not remove itself from unwanted public scrutiny. Subsequently it did little to endear itself to its constituents and its public. Players were allowed increasingly little scope to determine their own actions, and there were frequent disputes about payment. Ironically, one of the toughest members was reputed to be was Sir Donald Bradman.

On the other side of the world the MCC remained the government of cricket and retained many if not all its old standards. It was 1965, for example, before the ICC established at the height of Empire in 1909 was transformed into the International Cricket Conference, recognising in a token way at least a new political order. The Club continued as a major social institution with access to political power and influence. Its post-war presidents included the Duke of Edinburgh (1949 and 1974), Field Marshal Earl Alexander (1955), Sir William Worsley, Bt (1961), and Sir Alec Douglas-Home, Conservative Prime Minister (1966). Though shaken by the bodyline crisis, the MCC was not challenged as the premier cricket body—at least, not until the tumultuous days of the Packer revolution in 1977.

However, cricket's imperial links were never quite the same after bodyline. Attempts were made to sustain the 'cricket and empire' theme, especially between England and Australia, but the growing *need* to win as opposed to the *desire* to win of earlier decades helped undermine its symbolic meaning. Even by August 1933 a South African memorandum to a British Commonwealth Relations conference was dated in arguing that by the twenty-first century it would be important 'to know whether people in Capetown and Melbourne and Ottawa will still be reaching *Punch*, and whether cricket will still be played under the same rules at Lord's and Sydney'.

One measure of the imperial anxiety to heal the Anglo-Australian wounds inflicted by bodyline came in May 1933. Ernest Crutchley wrote to the Dominions Office about the 1934 tour of Victoria by the Prince of Wales to mark that state's centenary. He reported that Prime Minister Lyons thought a full federal tour rather than a restricted one would be of great value in the restoration of normality.

The Menzies papers in the Australian National Library contain some interesting relics of that attempt to sustain the old order, particularly in the proceedings of the South Australian Country Cricket Association. In 1949 the speech and toast to 'The British Empire and Cricket' at the annual dinner was delivered by premier Sir Thomas Playford (as he became) and Sir Willoughby Norrie, then state Governor and later Governor-General of New Zealand. In 1950 Sir Walter Duncan, so much involved at the Adelaide end of bodyline politics, spoke to 'The Commonwealth of Cricket'. The subtle language change was revealing.

By 1947, when Pakistan emerged as a new cricket nation after the partition of India, the British Empire was on the point of break-up. In some areas cricket became a symbol of colonial bondage as much as of imperial unity. Just one example of the link between cricket and late-colonial politics occured in the 1946 Indian tour, when Dr Subbaroyan, President of the Indian Board of Control and a former minister in the Madras Presidency, sought from his manager two copies of the latest White Paper on the British Cabinet Mission to India. The disastrous 1953–54 MCC tour of the West Indies foundered as much on the political situation in which it took place as on the personalities involved. An attempt at West Indian federation caused considerable tension between islands and against Britain—cricket disturbances accentuated the difficulties. From then on, in India, Pakistan, the West Indies and elsewhere, cricket has been an agent of Commonwealth dissension as well as of unity. The political use of cricket by Zulfikar Ali Bhutto's widow in Pakistan, the cancelled test in Guyana during the 1981 tour because of Robin Jackman's South African connections, and the illwill created between New Zealand and Australia over the underarm bowling incident are just three recent examples.

Until his death Sir Robert Menzies attempted to hold firm against these changes. His trips to England invariably involved cricket watching and gathering old cricketers (often adversaries) together at his famous dinners. His speeches, political or otherwise, were redolent of a past age of unity, though the substance was thinner than before. The Pacific War of 1942–45 had put Australia firmly into the American sphere and England now had a cultural rival in the Australian psyche. Postwar politics were generally unkind to cricket's imperial ideology.

In a wider sense bodyline may be regarded as the first major 'sport and politics' crisis in modern times. The sequences of events outlined in this book reveal at once the extent of that crisis and the reason for its long secrecy. The political events were kept extremely private by those most directly involved, so that the players had no knowledge of them and despite the presence of a large press contingent little if any of the political bargaining emerged in the public sphere. Not that British government departments were entirely without experience in sports issues which became political. The Dominions Office, for example, had worked on some soccer matters concerning the Irish Free State during 1930, and in the same period the Foreign Office registers show a steady increase in the political use of sport, especially concerning the growth of Fascism in Germany and Italy. However, bodyline was the biggest issue to date and potentially the most damaging. It also marked the beginning, or the consolidation, of an attitude which still bedevils attempts to see sport and politics in a rational way—that sport and politics should not mix, that somehow sport is 'different' from other avenues of life by being completely detached from its social context. Of course, bodyline revealed the opposite, that sport *could* damage wider international relations. That lesson was not learned, however, and governments found it increasingly difficult to handle sporting matters as sport became symbolically more important in the international arena.

Towards the end of 1935, for example, the Home Office and Foreign Office in Britain became embroiled in a complicated discussion concerning an England versus Germany soccer match held in London. Key figures in the Foreign Office, as archival documents reveal, were beginning to push for a hardline policy towards Hitler's Germany. Despite the presence of 10 000 Strength Through Joy movement Nazi supporters at the game, the government view remained that the affair was not political. That stance persisted during the 1936 Berlin Olympics debate in Britain. Although the British ambassador to Germany told his superiors that the Games *were* 'political', his advice was ignored. Interestingly enough, one of the key figures in this debate was a member of the 1932–33 MCC Committee, Lord Aberdare. Not only was he a leading member of the British Olympic Committee, he was also prominent in the Anglo-German Fellowship which employed cultural institutions like music and sport to create better relations between the two countries, so countering the Foreign Office line.

In these and other instances throughout the 1930s, sport and politics were naively thought separate. The trend continued apace after 1945. Although numerous world organisations excluded Germany and Japan from their sports councils on government advice, those governments still argued for the separation of sport and politics. The rise of superpower sports contests after the Soviet Union's 1952 appearance at the Olympics meant simply that the debate became more complex, with many government still trying to 'keep politics out of sport'. Despite the Suez crisis complications for the 1956 Olympic Games, the rise of sporting boycotts against South Africa, the Munich Massacre of 1972 which sprang out of Middle East politics and the growing government funding of sport for internationally symbolic purposes, many nations still thought that sport and politics *could* be separated. Even the attempted boycott of the 1980 Moscow Games by Western powers failed to drive home to some that sport is fundamentally political.

In 1932–33, however, all these developments lay ahead, unanticipated by authorities, players or public. As the world drifted towards a new war, England and Australia met each other three more times: Australia won two to one and three to two in 1934 and 1936–37, with the 1938 series drawn at one all. That was the final heyday of imperial cricket. As in 1914–18, the Second World War took a heavy toll of cricketers, including eleven test players. Those who survived returned to a very different world. That in itself was one of the reasons why bodyline subsided in the popular consciousness; it seemed unimportant after six years of war in which the imperial body stood firm. Yet, as the current interest in bodyline suggests, the MCC tour of Australia in 1932–33 remains a major benchmark in the evolution of Anglo-Australian imperial relations and social attitudes.

Sources

ARCHIVES The files and committee minutes of the Australian Cricket Board and the MCC were the starting points in our research. Much other significant material was found in the Australian Archives, Canberra; the Australian National Library, Canberra; the British Library, London; the Public Records Office, London; the State Archives of South Australia, Adelaide; and the La Trobe Library, Melbourne.

PRIVATE PAPERS The Viscount Bruce papers in the Australian Archives; the Hugh Buggy papers, La Trobe Library, Melbourne; the diary and letters of Ernest Crutchley held privately in England by Brooke Crutchley; the papers of Sir Walter Duncan and J.G. Duncan-Hughes, the State Archives of South Australia; and the collections of Sir John Latham, Sir Keith Officer and Sir Robert Menzies in the Australian National Library.

NEWSPAPERS AND PERIODICALS From Britain we consulted the Manchester *Guardian, Daily Herald, Daily Mail, Morning Post, Observer, Daily Telegraph, The Times*, London *Evening Standard* and London *Evening News*, plus the weekly *New Statesman & Nation*.

In Australia our research led us to the *Australasian*, Adelaide *Advertiser*, Brisbane *Courier Mail, Bulletin*, Melbourne *Age*, Melbourne *Argus*, Melbourne *Herald*, Sydney *Mail*, *Sydney Morning Herald*, Sydney *Referee*, *Smiths Weekly* and *West Australian*.

Wisden, the *Cricketer* and the *Australian Cricketer* all are essential references. The *Wisden Anthology 1900–1940*, edited by Benny Green, reprints virtually all the material from *Wisden* on bodyline, including all the cables. The *New South Wales Cricket Association Year Books* for 1932–33 and 1933–34 contain a detailed account of the tour and the exchanges between the MCC and the Australian Board.

Bibliography

Place of publication is London unless stated otherwise.

On bodyline

Blundell, R.W. *Bodywhine. A Treatise on the Jardinian Theory* Adelaide: Rigby, 1933

Corrie, R.T. *The Barracker at Bay: An outspoken reply to the Bodyliners* Melbourne: Keating-Wood, 1933

Docker, E.W. *Bradman and the Bodyline Series* Brighton: Angus & Robertson, 1978

Fingleton, J.H. *Cricket Crisis* Cassell, 1946

Glover, T. *Owzat. Tom Glover's Cricket Book* Sydney: Angus & Robertson, 1932

Harris, B. *Jardine Justified, The Truth about the Ashes* Chapman & Hall, 1933

Hobbs, J.B. *The Fight for the Ashes 1932-33* Harrap, 1933

Jardine, D.R. *In Quest of the Ashes* Hutchinson, 1933

Kippax, A.F. *Anti Body-Line* Sydney: Sydney & Melbourne Publishing Company, 1933

Larwood, H. *Body-Line? An Account of the Test Matches between England and Australia 1932-33* Mathews & Marrot, 1933

Larwood, H. with Perkins, K. *The Larwood Story* W.H. Allen & Co., 1965

Le Quesne, L. *The Bodyline Controversy* Secker & Warburg, 1983

Mailey, A.A. *And Then Came Larwood. An Account of the Test Matches 1932-33* John Lane, The Bodley Head, 1933

Man in the Street, *The Sporting English? From Front Line to Body Line* Sydney: MacQuarie Head Press, 1933

Mason, R. *Ashes in the Mouth* Hambledon Press, 1982

Stoddart, B. 'Cricket's Imperial Crisis: The 1932-33 MCC Tour of Australia' in Cashman, R. & McKernan, M. (eds) *Sport in History. The Making of Modern Sporting History* St Lucia: University of Queensland Press, 1979

Wilmot, R.W.E. *Defending the Ashes 1932-33* Melbourne: Robertson & Mullens, 1933

Wright, W.R. *Souvenir of English Cricketer's Visit to Adelaide* Adelaide: Osborne, 1933

Cricket and Empire

On cricket

Altham, H.S. and Swanton, E.W. *A History of Cricket* 4th edn, George Allen & Unwin, 1948

Ames, L.E.G. *Close of Play* Stanley Paul, 1953

Barty-King, H. *Quilt Winders and Pod Shavers: The History of Cricket Bat and Ball Manufacture* MacDonald & Jane's, 1979

Birley, D. *The Willow Wand* MacDonald & Jane's, 1979

Bowen, R. *Cricket. A History of its Growth and Development Throughout the World* Eyre & Spottiswoode, 1970

Bowes, W.E. *Express Deliveries* Stanley Paul, 1949

Bowes, W.E. 'Jardine D.R.' in Arlott, J. (ed.) *Cricket The Great Captains* Pelham Books, 1971

Bradman, D.B. *Don Bradman's Book* Hutchinson, 1930

—— *My Cricketing Life* Stanley Paul, 1938

—— *Farewell to Cricket* Hodder & Stoughton, 1950

Brodribb, G. *Maurice Tate* London Magazine Editions, 1976

Carr, A.W. *Cricket with the Lid Off* Hutchinson, 1935

Cashman, R. The Bradman Factor, essay available at the New South Wales Cricket Association Library

—— *Ave a Go Yer Mug. Australian Cricket Crowds* from Larrikin to Ocker Sydney: William Collins, 1984

Coldham, J.D. *Lord Harris* George Allen & Unwin, 1983

Downer, S. *100 Not Out. A Centenary of Cricket on the Adelaide Oval* Adelaide: Rigby, 1972

Fender, P.G.H. *Kissing the Rod. The Story of the Tests of 1934* Chapman & Hall, 1934

Ferguson, W.H. (as told to D.R. Jack) *Mr Cricket* Nicholas Kaye, 1957

Frith, D. *The Fast Men. A 200 year cavalcade of speed bowlers* 2nd edn, George Allen & Unwin, 1982

Hawke, M.B. *Recollections and Reminiscences* Williams & Norgate, 1924

Hobbs, J.B. *Recovering the 'Ashes': An account of the cricket tour in Australia, 1911–12* Pitman, 1912

James, C.L.R. *Beyond a Boundary* Hutchinson, 1963

Jardine, D.R. *Ashes and Dust* Hutchinson, 1934

—— *Cricket—how to succeed* Evans, 1936

—— *Cricket* J.M. Dent, 1949

MacLaren, A.C. *Cricket old and new* Longmans Green, 1924

Mailey, A.A. *10 for 66 And All That* Shakespeare Head, 1958

Marshall, J. *Lord's* Pelham Books, 1969

Moyes, A.G. *Bradman* Harrap, 1948

—— *Australian Cricket. A History* Sydney: Angus & Robertson, 1959

Noble, M.A. *Gilligan's Men: A critical review of the MCC tour of Australia, 1924–25* Chapman & Hall, 1925

—— *The Fight for the Ashes, 1928–29. A critical account of the English tour in Australia* Harrap, 1929

Bibliography

Oldfield, W.A. *Behind the Wicket. My Cricketing Reminiscences* Hutchinson, 1938

Page, M. *Bradman. The Illustrated Biography* Melbourne: MacMillan, 1983

Pollard, T. *Australian Cricket. The Games and the Players* Sydney: Hodder & Stoughton, 1982

—— *Pictorial History of Australian Cricket* Melbourne: J.M. Dent, 1983

Ranjitsinhji, K.S. *The Jubilee Book of Cricket* 6th edn, Edinburgh: Blackwood, 1898

—— *With Stoddart's team in Australia* Bowden, 1898

Richardson, V.Y. *The Vic Richardson Story: The Autobiography of a Versatile Sportsman* Adelaide: Rigby, 1967

Robinson, R. *Between Wickets* William Collins, 1946

—— *The Wildest Tests* Pelham Books, 1973

Rogerson, S. *Wilfred Rhodes. Professional and Gentleman* Hollis & Carter, 1960

Rosenwater, I. *Sir Donald Bradman* Batsford, 1979

Sharp, M. Professionalism and Commercialism in Australian Cricket during the 1930s: The Origins of the Cricket Revolution, University of New South Wales BA essay, available at the NSW Cricket Association Library, 1981

Streeton, R. *P.G.H. Fender* Faber & Faber, 1981

Sutcliffe, H. *For England & Yorkshire* Edward Arnold, 1935

Swanton, E.W. *Sort of A Cricket Person* William Collins, 1972

—— *Follow On* William Collins, 1977

Swanton, E.W. (ed.) *Barclays World of Cricket. The Game from A to Z* William Collins, 1980

Trevor, P.C.W. *With the MCC in Australia (1907–08)* A. Rivers, 1908

Verity, H. *Bowling 'em out* Hutchinson, 1936

Warner, P.F. *Cricket in Many Climes* Heinemann, 1900

—— *How we recovered the Ashes* Chapman & Hall, 1904

—— *Imperial Cricket* London & Counties Press Association, 1912

—— *Cricket Between Two Wars* Chatto & Windus, 1942

—— *Lord's 1787–1945* Harrap, 1946

Whitington, R.S. *The Time of the Tiger. The Bill O'Reilly Story* Stanley Paul, 1972

Whitington, R.S. and Hele, G. *Bodyline Umpire* Adelaide: Rigby, 1974

Wild, R. *The Biography of Colonel His Highness Shri Sir Ranjitsinhji Vibhaji, Maharaja Jam Saheb of Nawangar* Rich & Cowan, 1934

Wyatt, R.E.S. *Three Straight Sticks* Stanley Paul, 1951

Index